Bichon Frise

A Bichon Frise
Pet Owner's Guide

Bichon Frise Basics, Choosing and Owning,
Breeding, Care, Nutrition, Grooming, Showing and
Training All Included!

By: Lolly Brown

Foreword

Reading this instructional guide prior to buying or picking up your puppy will prepare you, benefit your new puppy and help you to establish the precise mindset for owning a Bichon Frise.

Included inside this book's first section is about the origin and bio of a Bichon Frise. It also contains information about its breed appearance, temperament and possible problem behaviors.

The Second section is about choosing a Bichon Frise. It tackles about where and how to acquire a Bichon Frise and how to select a healthy Bichon Frise puppy.

The next section will help you be prepared for your new puppy- the things that you need and have to do.

The fourth section focuses on how you can cater your dog's nutritional needs.

The fifth section is about raising and training your Bichon Frise. It educates dog owners about the importance of training and activities for your dog. It additionally contains a puppy's training outline and guidance in shaping behaviors, training, and problem solving.

The next section delves into basic care and regular grooming needs for your Bichon Frise.

Th seventh section focuses on the common health issues and how to deal with them and respond into emergencies.

Next is about preparing your Bichon Frise for a dog show.

The ninth section will guide you about the breeding process for your Bichon Frise.

For the last section, it will talk about the other care needs of your dog and how you will be able to deal with them.

By obtaining this training guide, you will be on your way to securing the necessary tools and knowledge to assure your success as a dog owner and trainer.

Table of Contents

Introduction

Before you can decide whether a Bichon Frise is the right pet for you, you need to learn the basics about this breed. In this book, you will receive a wealth of Bichon Frise information. By the time you finish this book, you should have a good understanding of what the Bichon Frise breed is like and you will be on your way to deciding if this is the right pet for you and your family.

For the most part, Bichon Frises are a friendly and playful breed, eager to spend time with family. Although these dogs do require a moderate amount of daily exercise, they are pretty good at entertaining themselves in the house as long as they have enough toys to play with. These dogs are very social as well and they love to be in the company of people and other dogs – they also tend to get along well with children.

The Bichon Frise dog breed is definitely a companion breed. These dogs crave human attention and they tend to bond closely with their owners. Bichon Frise are loyal and affectionate, eager to please their owners. This breed is also fairly intelligent and quick to learn. This makes tasks like house-training and obedience training relatively easy. As is true for all dogs, however, it is best that you start your dog with training and socialization as early as possible to prevent the development of behavior problems.

As this breed is so people-oriented, it is not recommended that you leave them alone for long periods of time without another dog to keep them company. This breed needs daily physical exercise as well as mental stimulation/interactive play, every-day. Failure to provide this type of stimulation can potentially to lead to behavioral problems relating to frustration and separation anxiety. This is likely to manifest itself with destructive or aggressive behavior. It is therefore not the dog's fault, but the owner's for not providing basic necessities such as daily exercise.

Let's get started!

Chapter One: Bichon Frise Origin

History

This breed hailed from the Mediterranean and they descended from a combination of Water Spaniels and Poodles. Also, it is perceived that Italian and Spanish sailors found these dogs and then brought them around the globe on their journey, at times using them to exchange for other goods. Eventually, this breed was appearing together with their royal owners in Renaissance paintings. It was in the late 1800s when this type of dog was regarded as common show dogs; however, it was in the year 1934, Bichons returned to popularity after they were recognized by the French Kennel Club. This breed flourished due to their charming personality and tiny size.

It was around the 19th century when Bichons had come down. It was in this time they started accompanying organ grinders, and they also performed on the street to amuse people or passersby while a few of this breed were renowned circus dogs. Bichons are also known to be a royal favorite, probably because of their clownish attributes. This breed also held valuable tasks and that is leading blind people.

Likewise, Bichons had a reputation for being a very exceptional companion. It was in the early 20th century when French breeders took them and wrote a breed standard for Bichons, and it was also in this period when the name Bichon Frise was given to them. This new name means "curly coat."

In the year 1956, a French family who moved to Michigan brought this breed with them. It was at this time the Bichons reached the United States of America. It was in the year 1964 when the Bichon Frise Club of America was founded. It is worth mentioning that the Bichon is actually ranked 37th in the class of breeds registered by the American Kennel Club, and in 2000, they became ranked 25th. Surely, Bichons will remain among the most fair-haired dogs.

This breed is described as a small-framed pooch that has soft, white, and fluffy coat. After several centuries of development in the land of Europe, this type of dog has become a very adorable and fond addition to countless of families at present.

Physical Characteristics

This is a very small dog breed. They have a very dense, soft, and double coat. One good thing about the coat is that it continues to grow without shedding much. To prevent matting, the owner should be deeply engrossed in frequent grooming.

Since it doesn't shed much, it is considerably a perfect breed for people with allergies. Generally, Bichon Frise dogs have a white coat. It can also be apricot or cream, grey and buff. Height for males is about nine up to twelve inches or twenty-three up to thirty centimeters, while females are about nine up to eleven inches or twenty-three up to twenty-eight centimeters. On the other hand, the weight is approximately three up to five kilograms or seven to twelve pounds. The lifespan is between 12 to 18 years.

Temperament

The temperament is evidenced by his dark-eyed impressive expression and plumed tail usually carried over the back. One of the remarkable traits of Bichon Frise dogs is a cheerful attitude. The dog has a winning personality, this is why it wants to be the center of attraction at all times and is adept at charming his neighbors, veterinarians, groomers and owner's family.

He doesn't like to be alone due to his playful attitude. If left alone for a few hours, you will discover that he will suffer from separation anxiety, and it can tear up, chew or destroy anything in sight. Indeed, Bichon is not recommended for people who are usually away from home for a long time (although no dog is).

Bichon is highly intelligent, bold, energetic and extremely playful. Thus, it yearns to be taught. The owner should teach him all the essentials of canine manners and obedience training. They have a high level of comprehension, so it could be a pleasure and hugely satisfying if you can take them to such classes. They are also very good in canine sports and tricks.

Their temperament is affected by a whole lot of factors including socialization, training and heredity. Puppies with temperament are playful in nature, curious, willing to stay with people, and held by them at the same time.

Like every other dog, Bichon needs early exposure or socialization to many people, sounds, sights and experiences especially while growing up. Early socialization makes sure that the dogs become well-rounded dog. You can kick start his exposure by enrolling him in a kindergarten class, taking him to busy stores, parks that allow dogs, inviting guests at intervals and on leisure strolls to meet new friends, neighbors, and family members- all these activities will end up polishing his social skills.

Incredibly, Bichon is a social dog that wants to interact with others, and they easily get along with other dogs, animals and children. The American Kennel Club recommends it as a dog that is 'cheerful, merry, affectionate, playful, sensitive and gently mannered.' He loves your company and would demand much from you. They can become very territorial if they are enshrined in a particular territory for a period of time.

Common Behaviors of Bichon Frise

- Bichons are usually very difficult to potty train or housebreak. One must be very patient and consistent enough at the time you're housebreaking this breed. They are very smart but this breed is not often very cooperative in terms of housebreaking.
- Since this type of dog is regarded as a slow maturing breed, it is harder to housebreak and it actually takes longer to housebreak them as compared to other breeds out there. As a matter of fact, at times, they are not 100% housebroken. Take into account that it requires more effort, more time, and a great deal of patience and determination to housebreak this breed.
- Bichons usually have lots of accidents. If you think that this will bother you, then never consider getting a Bichon Frise for you. If you're always out, then, this breed is not suitable for you. Bichons require getting out at least every two hours.

- Even though Bichon Frise possesses a great temperament and is known to be not harmful to children, this type of dog does not bond quite well with young kids. This breed prefers an adult's attention. Bichons know who is in charge, and that is the person to whom they seek attention to. Just like your child who wants your attention, the Bichon requires your attention too. It is advisable for parents to supervise their young kids primarily when playing with this small dog to make certain that kids do not hurt or do any harm to the puppy.
- Bichons are very dependent breeds. This breed is always under your feet, on your lap or in your face. They call for a great deal of love and attention and they can make their owners feel guilty, particularly when they're not able to provide them this kind of affection and attention.
- This breed is a little white and fluffy pooch that craves for human company. It possesses a very self-reliant spirit, very lively and bold.
- It is a gentle and charming dog yet is not a babbler. It has a confident and happy temperament which is unquestionably very easy to live with.
- Bichons may be trained easily since they are known to be brilliant dogs; no wonder why they are adored by many.
- Bichon Frise is not specifically fitted to live outside and must be an indoor pooch since it is very dedicated to the family.

- This breed is naturally friendly and sociable, and they are delighted when they're part of a family who takes them anywhere.
- This breed adapts well with other animals or pets once they are introduced slowly or reared with them. Bichons cope with both other dog breeds and cats very well.
- They are used to perform some amusing tricks and also used as watchdogs. They are very obedient and competitive.
- Bichons need some restrictions to what they are and not permitted to do and they also require some rules to adopt. They also necessitate pack walks every day.

Possible Problem Behaviors of Bichon Frise

- Never allow this little pooch to develop what is called small dog syndrome. This refers to a human-induced behavior in which the pooch feels that he is a pack leader to people. Eventually, this may lead to differing degrees of a broad array of behavior issues, comprising of, but not restricted to, separation anxiety, guarding, obsessive barking, biting, and snapping.
- It is significant to note that these are not Bichon attributes but behaviors induced by the way the puppy is treated. In the event that you begin to be your puppy's pack leader and you're constantly self-confident, assertive, and calm toward the puppy, giving it pack walk every day; then, this breed will be trustworthy and stable-minded.

- A Bichon Frise is typically a bit tough to housebreak.
- Some Bichons are known to be barky, and some of them also possess high-pitched bark, which may be annoying or disturbing.
- They are prone to separation anxiety. Most of this breed is quite reliant on human companionship, and they are sociable. So, as a consequence, once they are left alone for long periods of time.

Chapter Two: Choosing a Bichon Frise

Purchasing Your New Pet

There are multiple ways to purchase a dog: from a breeder, a pet store, or a rescue service. There are pros and cons of each method, and they will be explained in the following section.

Breeders

When it comes to purchasing a Bichon Frise, breeders are unarguably the best method. A breeder will allow you to interact with your Bichon Frise before you purchase it. This will allow you to understand the Bichon Frises temperament and behavior and allow you to inspect the Bichon Frise for any genetic defects. Breeders are usually a part of a registered service – such as The Kennel Club. By being a member of a registered organization, it gives the breeder accountability and legitimacy. Breeders will inform you of any issues with the Bichon Frise and how they have been socializing it. Breeders will also be able to tell you the exact birthdate of your new Bichon Frise. The only downside of breeders is that they are more expensive than pet stores – however, this should not be an issue when considering purchasing a Bichon Frise.

Pet Stores

Pet stores are a common choice when purchasing a new Bichon Frise – but I HIGHLY do not recommend purchasing a Bichon Frise from a pet store! Most pet stores purchase their Bichon Frises from puppy mills. Puppy mills are notorious for breeding and raising their Bichon Frises in terrible conditions, leading to both behavioral and health problems. Employees at the pet store will most likely not be able to provide you with specific information about a Bichon Frise – they are unlikely to know its exact date of birth and health background. The pedigree of a Bichon Frise from a pet store is also questionable. Pet stores have a terrible return policy! It is not uncommon for a new owner not to have fully considered every aspect of owning a Bichon Frise and therefore return it. If you return a Bichon Frise to a breeder, you can be assured that the Bichon Frise will lead a happy life. However, if you return a Bichon Frise to a pet store, it will most likely be euthanized if it has grown older than a puppy because it is unlikely to sell.

Rescue

If you are an experienced Bichon Frise owner, you may consider getting a Bichon Frise from a rescue shelter. Most Bichon Frises from rescue shelters are free, and the shelter just wishes you to donate. It is important to remember that rescue Bichon Frises may have health or behavioral issues due to their turbulent lives. Bichon Frises in rescue shelters are also hardly ever puppies and tend to be middle-aged or older. However, getting your Bichon Frise from a rescue shelter allows you to give a Bichon Frise a better life than they would have had in the past. Most Bichon Frises that end up in shelters have been cruelly treated or abandoned, and by adopting one you are giving the animal a chance to experience life in a loving home.

Choosing a Reputable Breeder

Once you have decided that the Bichon Frise is the right breed for you, you must take on the task of choosing a reputable breeder. Not only do you need to do some research, such as the recommended breeders above, to find a good breeder, but you also need to speak to the different breeders to determine which breeder is the best. The responsible Bichon Frise breeder will be careful about selecting healthy breeding stock and keeping detailed records of their breeding practices. If the breeder does not appear to be experienced with the Bichon Frise breed or breeding dogs in general, you should look elsewhere.

In addition to the above recommendations, try asking around at your local animal shelter or a veterinarian's office for their recommendations. Because the Bichon Frise is rapidly becoming a popular breed, there may be a breeder in your area that you do not know about. If neither of these options turns up any breeders, try looking in the phone book or perform an additional online search. Once you have compiled a list of several breeders, you can then go through the list to determine which one is the best option.

Follow the steps below to choose a reputable Bichon Frise breeder:

- Visit the website for each breeder, if they have one, and look for important information like photos of the facilities, the breeder's experience.
- Contact each breeder by phone and ask them questions about their experience with breeding and with Bichon Frises. If the breeder is hesitant to answer your questions or do not seem knowledgeable and experienced, move on to the next option.
- Evaluate the breeder's interest in learning more about you. A reputable breeder will not just sell his puppies to anyone; they should be eager to ask you questions to see if you are a good fit for one of their puppies.
- Narrow your list down to two or three breeders that seem to be a good fit and visit the facilities before you commit to buy a puppy.

- Ask for a tour of the facilities and look to make sure that the dogs are kept in clean conditions and appear to be in good health.
- Make sure you see the breeding stock for the puppies available to make sure that they are in good health and purebred specimens of the Bichon Frise breed.
- Ask to see the available puppies and make sure that they are kept in clean conditions. If they are under 6 weeks of age, the puppies should be kept with the mother.
- Choose the breeder that you feel is most knowledgeable and experienced, as well as the one that has puppies available.
- Ask about the process for reserving a puppy. You will probably have to leave a deposit by way of a down payment. In addition, ask what comes with the puppy (vaccinations, worming, etc.).
- A reputable breeder will offer some kind of health guarantee on the puppy as well as information about the parents to certify its breeding.

Selecting a Healthy Bichon Frise Puppy

After you have gone through the process of selecting a reputable Bichon Frise breeder, your next step is to choose a healthy puppy. While it may be tempting to buy the first Bichon Frise puppy that comes up to you with a wagging tail, you need to be a little more cautious about the process. Taking the time to ensure that the puppy is in good health could save you a lot of veterinary bills (not to mention heartache) in the future.

Follow the steps below to pick a healthy Bichon Frise puppy:

- Ask to see all of the puppies at once and spend a few minutes watching how they interact with each other before you approach them.
- Healthy puppies should be playful and energetic, and should not be acting lethargic.
- Make yourself available to the puppies but do not immediately try to interact. Wait and see which ones are curious enough to approach you.
- Bichon Frise puppies are very energetic and playful, so they should be eager to interact with you.
- Spend a few minutes engaging with each puppy. Play with a toy to gauge the puppy's activity and try petting him to make sure he doesn't respond with fear or aggression.
- If you can watch the puppies being fed as well, to make sure that they have a healthy appetite. A puppy that does not eat is likely to be sick.
- Examine the puppies more closely for signs of good health. Do not just look for obvious signs of illness.

Below is a list of what you should look for in different categories:

- Eyes: bright and clear; no discharge or crust
- Breathing: quiet and steady; no snorting, coughing, or sneezing

- Energy: alert and energetic; eager to play
- Body: The puppy should look well-fed, not too skinny
- Genitals: the genitals should be clean
- Coat: the coat should be clean and healthy without bare patches, flaking skin, or other problems; the color should be uniform
- Gait: the puppy should move quickly without limping or evidence of soreness/stiffness
- Hearing: the puppy should react if you clap your hands behind his head
- Vision: the puppy should be able to see clearly if you toss a toy or roll a ball across his line of sight

If the puppies appear to be physically healthy and do not show any behavioral warning signs like aggression, excessive fear, or lethargy, they are probably a good buy. Once you've assessed the puppies' condition, you can spend some more time playing with them to find out which puppy is a good personality match for you. Keep in mind that your puppy's personality and temperament might change a little as he grows, but you have some control over that, depending on how you train and socialize him over the coming weeks.

Chapter Three: Owning a Bichon Frise

Dog Equipment Basics and Essentials

Before purchasing a Bichon Frise, it is essential to make sure that you have already purchased all the equipment you will need to provide your new Bichon Frise with the best possible care. Ensuring you have all the essential equipment before purchasing your pet is the best way to build a strong relationship with your pet and keep it content, happy, and healthy.

Collars and ID Tags

Purchasing a collar with an ID tag is arguably one of the most important things you can purchase for your Bichon Frise. The collar allows you to attach a leash to your Bichon Frise, which allows you to take your pet for a walk, which is essential to their health. There is a wide range of collars available to purchase made from multiple different materials and styles. It is essential to take your dog's habits into account when purchasing a collar. For example, if your dog regularly enjoys swimming, it is not advisable to purchase a leather collar. It is also important not to purchase a thin collar! When you walk your Bichon Frise on a leash, it may lunge, or pull, which will cause the collar to dig into its neck. I recommend having your Bichon Frise's name and your home address on the ID tag. This will allow the person who finds your dog to keep it calm by using its familiar name and will know where to return your pet to.

Leashes and Harnesses

Purchasing a lead or harness is vital in ensuring your Bichon Frise remains healthy! Having a lead or harness allows you to walk your pet and provide them with the exercise they need. Walking your pet also helps to create a strong bond and friendship between the two of you. There are a few differences between Leashes and Harnesses, which will be explained below:

Leash: Most dog owners will use a leash while walking their pets. Leashes ensure both comfort and safety when you take your dog out for a walk. It is important to buy a leash that extends to allow your dog to explore and move away from you at times. It is equally important to buy a sturdy leash that will allow you to keep control of your pet for the entirety of the walk.

Harness: If you have a large, small, energetic, or boisterous dog, a harness may be a safer option. The harness is safer for these dogs as they will not feel discomfort from their collar when they pull against the leash. Purchasing a front-clip harness (that goes over the dog's chest) will allow you to have more control over your pet.

Bedding

Some owners allow their dogs to sleep in their beds or on their sofas. While this can be a great way to build a strong relationship with your dog it is also important to purchase a suitable bed for your pet. Providing your pet with its own bed will give your dog a place of its own to feel safe and secure.

There is an overwhelmingly wide variety of dog beds available in pet stores and on the internet. I recommend adhering to the following criteria when purchasing a dog bed to ensure practicality, safety, comfort and warmth.

- **Natural Materials:** It is important to make sure the dog bed you purchase is made of natural materials.

Synthetic products, including fire retardants and stain-proof chemicals, may be harmful to your dog's health.

- **Removable Cover:** If you purchase a dog bed with a removable cover, it allows you to regularly and easily clean your dog's bed. Keeping your pet's bedding clean is essential to keeping your pet healthy as it removes bacteria and any parasites that may have found their way into the bedding. Purchasing a bed with a removable cover also allows you to replace the cover if it keeps overly worn and ripped – replacing just the cover is a lot less expensive than replacing an entire bed!

- **Non-Skid Bottom**: When your dog dives into its bed, you do not want it to slide across the floor as this could damage your pet, the bed, and the floor. Purchasing a bed with a non-skid bottom removes the chance of injury and damages.

- **Plan Ahead**: If you are buying a puppy it is important to remember that your puppy will grow! It is considered best practice to purchase a bed that is the correct size for an adult dog to not be outgrown.

There are two main categories of beds that are suitable for dogs. It is important to watch your dog sleep so you have an idea of how its sleeping preferences and how it physically lies down. Choosing the correct bedding is vital to ensure your dog feels safe and secure at home. The two categories of bedding are as follows:

- Round / Nest-Style Beds: These beds are ideal for smaller dogs and larger dogs who like to curl up when they sleep.
- Raised / Cushion / Futon Beds: These beds are ideal for dogs who enjoy stretching themselves out when they sleep.

Food and Water Bowls

It is important to purchase a food bowl and a water bowl for your pet Bichon Frise. There are three primary materials that are used to create these bowls: plastic, ceramic, stainless steel. The following section will outline the pros and cons of each material.

- **Plastic:** Plastic bowls are cheap, durable, and long-lasting. The only downside of a plastic bowl is that plastic can be toxic to dogs if ingested. If you notice your dog gnawing at its bowl, you should replace it with either a ceramic or stainless-steel bowl.
- **Ceramic:** Ceramic bowls are very stable and heavy, which makes them a good choice if your dog pushes its bowl while it eats or drinks. The main downside of using a ceramic bowl is that they are porous and need to be thoroughly cleaned daily.
- **Stainless Steel:** Stainless Steel bowls are recommended by vets and dog care experts. They are easy to clean, easy to sanitize, durable and inexpensive. Similar to when purchasing a dog bed, it is considered best practice to purchase a

stainless-steel bowl with a non-skid bottom to prevent the bowl from moving while your dog eats or drinks.

Control for Worms, Ticks and Fleas

Part of your responsibility as a Bichon Frise owner is to control and kill the parasites that your Bichon Frise will definitely get at some point. Worms, Ticks, and Fleas can cause severe discomfort and health issues if left unchecked. There are medicated collars and shampoos that help minimize your Bichon Frise's chance of getting fleas and ticks. There are also medicines you can purchase to help prevent both external and internal parasites. It is considered best practice to take your pet to your local vet and ask them to give you a prescription for medicines to control parasites.

Toys

Toys for your Bichon Frise are essential for so many different reasons! Toys can provide your pet with mental and physical stimulation, which can also lead them to having less destructive behavior patterns – such as chewing up furniture! Chew toys can also have dental health benefits. Toys also allow you to build a strong and fun relationship with your pet. The following list details some of the most popular toys available on the market:

- Chew Toys: Chew toys can provide your dog with hours of solo fun and can also help your dog to develop a strong and healthy jaw. Before giving your dog a chew toy, it is important to check that it is not too hard – an overly hard chew toy can have the opposite effect and damage your dog's jaw! A good rule of thumb is to bang the chew toy on your knee – if it hurts, it is too hard for your dog's mouth! It is likewise important to make sure that your dog does not ingest any of the chew toys though as the plastic, or rubber, is toxic!

- Tug Toys: Tug toys are a very popular choice as they allow you to play with your dog actively. It is important not to allow your dog to become aggressive while you play with the tug toy! To avoid your dog becoming aggressive you should keep a positive and happy inflection in your voice. The most popular choices for tug toys are ropes and squishy plastic bones.

- Balls and Fetch Toys: Balls and fetch toys are another great way to play with your pet actively. It is important to purchase fetch toys made of soft plastic so your dog will suffer no dental damage or physical pain (if they miss the catch and get hit by the toy). Good choices for fetch toys are balls, Frisbees, cuddly toys, and squishy plastic sticks. Tennis balls are a common choice for fetch but are not actually a healthy choice of toy! The covering on Tennis balls can actually abrade the enamel on your dog's teeth, which can lead to serious health, and dental issues in later life.

- Food-Dispensing Toys: Food-dispensing toys are a great way to stimulate your dog mentally. They come in a variety of different styles and shapes. I recommended purchasing a ball or cube as it will also allow your dog to push the toy around which encourages physical activity as well.

Naming your puppy

If you have finally chosen the dog or puppy you want then perhaps now is as good a time as any to decide on his name. If you have hopefully bought from a reputable breeder and are leaving a deposit to collect him in a few weeks, you can get the breeder to start calling him by that name. Choosing your dog's name is exciting. Even an adult dog can learn a new name and some have no choice, arriving into rescue nameless. It is pretty easy to teach your dog his new name and considering how intelligent this breed is, the process should only take a few days. The idea is simply to show the dog that the sound of a certain word (his name or training command) means that he will need to pay attention, because you are speaking to him.

Eventually, your dog will know when he is being talked about just by the sound of his name. For now, though, you can offer him treats and say his name, plus call him between two people then use his name as he approaches. I simply say the name, give the dog a small treat and repeat this five or six times each session.

You can also prefix every positive interaction with your dog with his name. This way, he will learn it even quicker. Never use his name for anything negative or your dog will try his hardest not to respond when he hears it. Always make it lively and fun and soon your dog will know exactly who he is. You probably already have ideas yourself, but if not, please make the name short and sweet. Something like Daisy, Tess, Max or a name that relates to his appearance, such as Patch.

Puppy-Proofing Your Home

Depending on when you visit the breeder, the puppies may not be ready to take home just yet. As mentioned previously, a responsible breeder will not sell a puppy under 8 weeks old or until the puppies are fully weaned. Even if the puppies are available when you visit, you should wait until you have prepared your home before buying the puppy.

Below you will find some important steps to take in puppy-proofing your home:

Your Bichon Frise will want to explore every nook and cranny of his new home. Part of that process involves his teeth. Keep all items that are valuable or dangerous away from him. This particularly includes electrical cables that may be live, and therefore the puppy is risking an electric shock and, at worse, a fatality. Replace them with non-toxic chewable puppy toys in bright colors. Any chewed items are your responsibility, and you should be aware that the puppy may see lots of interesting things to chew. They do not see the value or the danger, so please be aware that it is not your

Bichon Frise's fault if something gets chewed. Never use harsh corrections. Not even a tap on the nose. Instead, use a firm "No" and replace the item with a chew-able dog toy made especially for teething pups.

Anywhere within your home that your Bichon Frise puppy is allowed to wander needs to be puppy-proofed. This is similar to baby-proofing your home, and requires you to go down on hands and knees and see what dangers lurk at puppy eye level.

Puppies enjoy chewing the solid rubberized covering of electrical cords and outlets. BE AWARE; these can result in your puppy getting a nasty shock, severely burned, or a fatality. Pups can also pull down electrical appliances by yanking on the cords.

- Prevent your Bichon Frise from jumping up on any unstable objects like bookcases.
- Do not allow your Bichon Frise access to high decks or ledges, balconies, open windows, or staircases. Instead use baby gates, baby plastic fencing and prevent accidents from happening.
- Never slam doors with a Bichon Frise puppy in the house. Use doorstops to make sure that the wind does not slam a door in your Bichon Frise's face.
- Clear glass doors also pose a danger since your Bichon Frise may not see them and run right into one. Use a screen door.
- Keep your doors securely shut and prevent an accident.

- Check for toxic plants, medicines, sharp objects, and even dead branches. Your Bichon Frise puppy could run right into something at breakneck Bichon Frise speed.
- The whole point of the preceding is to get you to think about any potential hazards for your Bichon Frise. Remember, they rely on you as their guardian, in much the same way as a child.

Toxins to Be Aware of in Your Home

- Insecticides
- Human medications
- Household cleaning products
- Foods that we consume that have a toxic effect on dogs such as grapes and chocolates
- Rodenticides
- Plants
- Garden and pool products
- Glass, razors, bathroom products
- Coins, small batteries, and other small objects that may easily be ingested

You'll need to oversee your Bichon Frise puppy for the first few months to make sure that he does not get into harm's way. Usually the kitchen is made into the puppy's room. In this instance, it's best to make sure that all cleaning supplies are removed and placed elsewhere. Bichon Frise pups are curious, and it can take as little as a few minutes for your puppy to get into a poisonous cleaning product.

Checking for Toxins in Puppy Toys

Before purchasing toys for your Bichon Frise to play with, you'll need to check that they are lead-free and cadmium-free.

Vulnerable puppies are at risk of been given chew toys that may contain lead and cadmium.

Studies from the University of Wisconsin-Madison demonstrate that all toxic responses to environmental pollutants appear in stressed animals. It's important to remove all environmental stressors from your Bichon Frise's life and to do all you can to prevent him from being isolated and succumbing to depression and anxiety.

Therefore, select chew toys that are free from lead and cadmium. Dog toys that contain DEHP- bis (2-ethylhexl) phthalate have been found to have a significant effect on the reproductive system of rats, even at very low doses. Toy products from Cordura like the Frisbee contain no detectable amounts of lead, cadmium, or phthalates. Use non-toxic tennis balls from Planet Dog or other reputable sources. These balls are not only indestructible; they are entirely free of phthalates and heavy metals.

Non-toxic play toys are very important for all Bichon Frise puppies that experience stress when left alone. These toys serve as anxiety busters and give your Bichon Frise puppy something to do when left alone.

Puppyhood does not last for very long and is a very special time in everyone's lives. During the puppyhood stage, training, playing, socializing, and all the preparation you do with your Bichon Frise puppy needs to be taken seriously.

Puppies need so much more than love. They also need you to keep them safe and out of trouble. Bichon Frise pups can get themselves into plenty of trouble. Every single interaction that you will have with your Bichon Frise puppy will be firmly imprinted. Meet your puppy's emotional needs first, then learn how to live successfully with your Bichon Frise by training and protecting him.

First Introductions

When you introduce your new Bichon Frise to everyone else in the household it's important to be careful and respectful of how everyone feels and may react.

If you are bringing home a young puppy, this will be easier because the puppy will generally accept anyone and everyone when carefully handled. In the case of bringing a puppy home the other animals in the family must be considered.

Some older dogs that you may already have, are completely overwhelmed by the new squeaking, face-licking, and over-keen puppy.

In the beginning, they may want to be nowhere near the baby dog. If you live with an older dog, ensure that he does not get walked on and harassed in those early days, particularly if he is worried. Similarly, take extra care with the cat and any other pets you may have.

If you are bringing home an older dog to a home with an existing dog, it is important to take all resources away that may cause friction. So, pick up toys, treats, and anything that either dog may guard. Remember that a new dog may feel insecure, therefore guard things for that reason alone.

It's a good idea to let two older dogs meet on neutral ground. At the park or somewhere similar, rather than just bring the new dog directly home. Walking them together first will allow them to get used to the scent of each other and do the 'meet and greet' without the tension of perceived territory.

Introducing Your Puppy to Children

Bichon Frises are a very social and people-oriented breed, so they tend to get along well with children. However, this doesn't mean that you can just put your puppy in a room with your kids and expect everything to be fine. Just as you need to ensure that your puppy is safe in your home, you also need to teach your kids how to properly handle the puppy for their own safety.

Introducing your children to the new dog is essential. The kids must learn that the dog is not a toy and a young puppy is very fragile. Never leave your children alone with a new Bichon Frise of any age as this could be risky for all of them. Carefully explain to your children as much information as you can from this book and you will find that the dog and children become friends for life.

Just as you do between two dogs, watch out for resource guarding between dogs and children. Kids tend to grab at toys and food bowls, particularly the little ones. A dog could easily see this behavior as a threat and snap in return. Similarly, remember that any dog will not appreciate uncomfortable poking and prodding before he tells the child to go away, in the only way that he can.

Do not allow your child to follow a dog that has tried to move away from the attention. This is a recipe for disaster because the dog can feel cornered and think he has to resort to aggression simply to be left alone.

If you manage your family well and teach all-around respect, you will be able to integrate the new dog perfectly and before you know it, everyone will be great friends.

Follow the tips below to safely introduce your puppy to children:

1.   Before you bring the puppy home, explain to your children how to properly handle the puppy. Tell them that the puppy is fragile and should be handled with care.
2.   Tell your children to avoid over-stimulating the puppy. They need to be calm and quiet when handling him so he does not become frightened.

3. When it is time to make introductions, have your children sit on the floor in your home and bring the puppy to them.

4. Place the puppy on the floor near your children and let the puppy wander up to them when he is ready. Do not let your children grab the puppy.

5. Allow your children to calmly pet the puppy on his head and back when he approaches them. You may even give them a few small treats to offer the puppy.

6. Let your children pick up the puppy if they are old enough to handle him properly. If the puppy becomes fearful, have them put him back down.

If the puppy becomes afraid at any point during your introductions, you should take him out of the situation and place him in his crate where he can feel safe. Do not let your children scream or act too excited around the puppy until he gets used to them. It will take time for both your children and your puppy to get used to each other and you should supervise all interactions.

Please do remember that where children are concerned or you already have a few pets, be extra careful of where your attentions go. After all, you want all of your pets to get along with each other, as well as your children. So do not create jealousy by fussing over your new Bichon Frise puppy and ignoring your other pets. Share your attention equally between all your pets so that the relationship starts well. Much of the future relationship between all of your pets will depend on what happens during the first few days.

With children in the picture, this new relationship must start well and gently. If your Bichon Frise puppy is your first puppy, as stated above, it's best to prepare young children with a firm explanation that all puppies need plenty of rest, quiet, and gentleness. Prepare them ahead of time by showing them how to touch a small puppy and what tone of voice to use, i.e., low and comforting.

Children should never scream or run around a small, vulnerable puppy. They also should not pull his ears, tail, or any other part of the puppy. It's best to be very firm about all the puppy rules ahead of time.

Where Will Your Puppy Sleep?

Deciding where your puppy will sleep is important. Many people choose to allow a little dog on their bed, which is fine. However, it's important to understand separation anxiety if you sleep with your dog and allow him to be with you at all times. Separation anxiety is caused by over-attachment, and sleeping in your bed can be part of the reason for that.

On the first night when you bring your puppy home, I suggest that you don't leave him alone. Imagine how he would feel after being in the warmth of his nesting area with his mother and siblings to be then completely alone. So make a conscious decision to stay in the room where your puppy will be sleeping for a couple of nights. You can also invest in a particular puppy comforter meant for the first few nights in a new home, they can be warmed in the microwave, and some even have heartbeats.

If your puppy will eventually be sleeping alone, then it's not a good idea to allow him to sleep on you. It would be much better to lie on the couch and have him on the ground beside you. That way, you can offer a comforting hand when needed, but he will be learning to leave behind the warmth of bodies at bedtime. You can introduce the crate right at the beginning if you prefer, or wait until that first couple of nights are over. Eventually, you will be able to leave a happily secure puppy in his sleeping place with ease.

An older dog that will be sleeping in another room, in the beginning will probably howl and bark for the first few nights. Do not panic, though, because this is often due to unsettled feelings rather than severe separation anxiety. It usually wears off when the dog begins to feel secure.

Chapter Four: Nutrition for Bichon Frise

There are so many different dog food brands available: organic, all-natural, hypo-allergenic, vegetarian, and even vegan! Good dog food is vital to provide your pet with the nutrition it needs to reach its full potential physically and mentally. Good nutrition helps your Bichon Frise fight disease, prevents obesity, minimizes your dog's chance of getting an illness, and generally improves your Bichon Frise's overall health and happiness. You should only feed your dog food that has been approved by the Association of American Feed Control (AAFCO) as it will ensure that the food is both safe and nutritious. You should look for brands of dog food that claim to have an 'AAFCO approved complete and balanced nutritional value' – it is illegal for a brand to claim that they have been approved by the AAFCO if they have not. Make sure the food you purchase contains protein, carbohydrates, fats, vitamins and minerals.

Changing Types of Food

Suppose you currently have your Bichon Frise on one type or brand of food and would like to change over to another type. In that case, there is a way to minimize the possibilities of upsetting his or her digestive tract and minimize the chance of refusal to eat the new food. This method includes gradually introducing small portions of the new food with the current food until the transition is complete. To change foods, simply follow these steps:

- Measure the full portion of original food, then remove approximately 1/5th to 1/4 of the amount and replace it with the new food.
- Place this in front of your Bichon and allow 15-20 minutes to finish eating. Remove the dish, even if your dog has not eaten or finished the food. Some picky eaters will initially refuse food. Do not punish or scold your dog or attempt to coerce them to eat by adding anything additional to the food dish (like gravy, milk or other enticing foods).
- Avoid feeding any treats until the next scheduled feeding time. Since most owners feed twice a day this should be in roughly twelve hours. Repeat the process by placing a new, fresh dish of 4/5 to 1/5 or ¾ to 1/4 food out for your Bichon. Most Bichons,

even those who are very particular eaters, will eat a bit of the mix. If they do not, repeat steps 2 and 3 but add additional, reasonable levels of exercise.

- Feed this mixture for a week or until your Bichon eats the required and correct amount within your 15-20 minute feeding period.
- The next week increase the mix to ½ and ½ original and new foods. Usually there will be no food refusal as your Bichon has already accepted the new food. Continue with this feeding mix for 5-7 days to allow the Bichon's system to ad- just.
- The third week, feed 1/4 original to ¾ new foods following the same pattern.
- At the end of the third week you should be able to feed 100% new food. This slow transition will prevent many of the possible diarrhea complications, constipation, or vomiting often associated with drastic and sudden changes in diet.

By keeping a Bichon on the same mixture of food for five to seven days between in- creases, it doesn't even realize that the switch has been made. Bichon Frises that are very picky eaters may need to go more than one feeding be- fore they start to eat the food mixture the first time. Owners need to be very firm in keeping treats, snacks and little food items away from their dog to encourage him or her to eat the correct food. Bichons that are used to a lot of human food and snacks can be very stubborn about eating only dog food. If you have any concerns about how long your Bichon is refusing food contact your vet for assistance.

Keeping a Routine

Establishing a routine for feeding your Bichon Frise is important to help your dog understand when food is coming and how long they have to eat. Most vets do not recommend free access to food, since many Bichons will simply over-eat leading to obesity and other digest problems. When there is more than one dog in the house, often free access food causes fights and aggression and even one dog refusing to allow the other access to their food. Often the dominant Bichon will guard the food and overindulge whereas the others will be underfed.

In addition, free access food doesn't allow the owner to monitor when their Bichon is eating properly until there is a significant change in physical indication. Professionals working with Bichon Frises recommend that these dogs have access to fresh, clean water at all times but only have access to their food for two fifteen to twenty-minute blocks in the day. If you have a Bichon that is prone to bloat you may be required to feed several smaller meals rather than the two medium sized portions. Bichons should not be strenuously exercised for at least an hour after eating, but a walk is completely acceptable. Puppies may require three or four feedings per day as recommended by the breeder or your vet.

Setting a routine for feeding is also important for housetraining and ensuring that there are no accidents or messes in the house. Most Bichons will need to go outside to toilet 20 to 30 minutes after eating, but each dog has their own timeframe. Feeding at least an hour before leaving the Bichon alone in the house will help with being able to feed your dog, let them relax, and then walk them or let them outside before they have to be left alone. Once the Bichon gets used to the routine, they will know what to expect and are much more likely to toilet when they need to, rather than after you leave. If your Bichon appears to be messing in the house the food may contain a high percentage of bulking agents and changing foods may correct the problem if this is the case.

How Much and What to Feed

Each type and brand of food will indicate on the bag or can how much to feed your Bichon Frise. Foods specially designed for small, medium or large breeds generally are the same food, just in different sized kibbles. Most dry foods will indicate a cup measure based on the body weight of your Bichon. Avoid foods that simply indicate to feed a set amount based on breed or small, medium, and large categories. Using the guidelines accurately will help prevent overfeeding and will also help with weight control and maintenance. Generally, most breeders, vets and handlers recommend that dry food only be fed to Bichon, unless there are special circumstances. Wet or canned foods tend to cause more digestive problems, cause dental problems in Bichon, as well as often cause diarrhea and overall poor health.

Canned foods often are difficult to measure and are much more challenging to understand based on label information. Occasionally older Bichon Frises, Bichons recovering from certain procedures, pregnant females or Bichons on special diets may require canned food as recommended by a vet. Never feed a Bichon Frise until he or she stops eating or leaves food in the dish. As mentioned above some Bichons will literally eat everything put in front of them rather than leave any food behind. You may notice that some brands have very different feeding levels.

Usually less expensive brands will have more fillers, seen as the top five ingredients on the label, and may include terms such as corn, wheat gluten, sorghum or cereal food. These items may contain some of the vitamins necessary for the Bichon but they are not important nutritionally in large quantities. To test what happens to your particular brand of dry dog food, place a small amount in a shallow dish of warm water for 15-20 minutes. When you return if the product is about the same size and still somewhat firm it is fairly easy for the Bichon to digest. If, when you return, it has expanded or swollen up and turned mushy that is exactly what it is doing in the Bichon's stomach. This is mostly an "empty" nutritional value food. Remember the more food in the more waste out. Read the food labels and look for an average protein base of at least 21% for less active Bichon or up to 26% for very active Bichons. The label will list both the ingredients and the analysis. While the ingredients are important, the analysis is really the key factor.

Making Your Own Bichon Frise Food

Some Bichon Frise owners prefer to make their own food. This is certainly an option, although it does take considerable time, effort, and a basic understanding of nutritional needs. One of the biggest difficulties in making your own food is ensuring that you are providing a nutritionally balanced diet with the correct amounts of:

- Carbohydrates
- Proteins
- Amino acids
- Vitamins
- Minerals
- Fats

Many of the recipes on the internet and in basic Bichon Frise care books indicate that they are balanced but, unless you have access to a laboratory or food analysis equipment, there is really little guarantee. Some breeders and even vets can provide nutritionally balanced recipes for dog food that are analyzed and are very healthy to feed your Bichon.

If you have a large Bichon or more than one Bichon, the sheer amount of time needed to prepare ingredients and actually cook the food may make it logistically impossible to make enough.

Remember that most homemade foods will have no preservatives, so will have a much shorter shelf-live than commercially available foods. Homemade dog food will also be more costly than commercially available foods. Since you are not buying in bulk as commercial dog food manufacturers do, you will pay more per pound for most meats and vegetables. If you do want to make your own dog food consider talking with your local butcher or grocery store to see if you can purchase trimmings or other items that may be less expensive than full cuts of meat.

Foods to Avoid

Sometimes people inadvertently feed their Bichon Frise food items that are simply not good for them. Occasionally, these foods may be fatal, even in small quantities. To avoid any problems with diets, avoid feeding the following:

Chocolate

Can be fatal even in small quantities.

Milk or milk products

In large quantities, it will cause diarrhea

Raw eggs

In large quantities can interfere with biotin absorption by the body. Cooked eggs are suitable for Bichons.

Grapes or raisins

Can be toxic to Bichons, even in small amounts

Raw or cooked fat

Can lead to diseases of the pancreas as well as digestive problems.

Human foods or table scraps

Leads to obesity and food refusal of balanced diets.

Liver

Too much raw or cooked liver can lead to Vitamin A toxicity

Nuts

Some nuts such as walnuts or macadamia nuts can cause seizures

Salt

Too much salt can lead to electrolyte imbalances

Sugar

Candies or sugary foods can lead to diabetes in Bichons as well as obesity.

Raw Garlic or Onions

Can be toxic to Bichons. Human foods are generally not acceptable for Bichon Frise, although they certainly enjoy them! Try to start your puppy off right by not feeding table scraps or human treats, instead purchase or make some nutritionally balanced dog treats and feed them sparingly.

Raw fish

May contain bacteria or can prevent thiamine absorption

Cat food

High in sugar, protein, and fat; can cause diarrhea and vomiting.

Weight and Diet

Often Bichon Frise owners are uncertain about what their Bichon actually weighs. Keeping a written journal of your Bichon's weight is a great idea. An easy way to chart this is to get the weight during the regular vet check-up. Watch your Bichon for signs of weight gain or loss in-between visits. To weigh a Bichon puppy at home, simply weigh yourself on a bathroom scale, step off, pick up the pup, and weigh yourself again. Subtract the two measures and the difference will be the weight of your Bichon. With their petite size, it may be possible to have the Bichon sit on the scale, or hold the Bichon on the scale. Most vets will allow you to come in and use the large, step on scales in their office provided that you call ahead. Another easy way to monitor large Bichons is simply using a string or measuring tape snugly around the abdomen or chest area. Record the measurement. You can determine if the Bichon has gained or lost weight by measuring again in the same spot, although you will not know the exact amount, pound wise. A breed-specific guideline for the average weights of a Bichon is also helpful.

Remember that this information is general and your Bichon may be slightly heavier or lighter depending on its physical size within the breed. Females will generally weigh slightly less than males but will also be physically smaller. Generally, the following applies:

Bichon Frises fall within the small size range with healthy females weighing in at 8 to 12 pounds and healthy males generally at 10 to 15 pounds.

A better way to determine if your Bichon Frise is the correct weight is to look at their overall condition. The following is a general description of the body condition that thin, healthy, and overweight Bichon Frise may exhibit:

Thin

Ribs, hips and backbone easily seen or felt through the coat. No fat or muscle mass over most of the Bichon's frame. Noticeable tuck up or angle between the chest and the abdomen.

Underweight

Some fat covering on ribs but minimal. Ribs are easily seen or felt through the coat. Noticeable tuck up at the abdomen. Some muscle mass but minimal. When viewed from above, the waist is dramatically noticeable and drawn in towards the backbone.

Ideal

Ribs covered with fat but still easily felt. Not easily seen when the animal is standing. Abdomen gently tucked up but in balance with the chest and hips. Muscles are evident. When view from the top, the waist is slightly curved toward the backbone.

Overweight

Ribs are covered with a noticeable fat layer. There is little difference between the chest level and the abdomen. The waist is not visible, and the Bichon looks square when view from above.

Obese

Ribs cannot be felt or seen. There is no difference between the ribs and the abdomen and the Bichon basically has a square profile when viewed from the top or the side. Some obese Bichons will have a distended stomach and abdomen.

Both underweight and overweight Bichons are at risk for health conditions such as heart and respiratory problems, as well as joint and muscle pains and arthritis. Keeping your Bichon within a healthy weight range will help them stay active even as they enter into their years as a senior Bichon.

Feeding Obese Bichon Frises

Feeding an obese Bichon is much the same as working on weight loss in humans. A combination of changes in diet and increasing exercise is the best possible option. To start a dietary change for an obese Bichon, first consult with your vet to ensure there are no other health conditions causing the weight problems. After your Bichon has a clean bill of health, start by decreasing the amount of food that you are feeding and increasing the amount of regular, supervised exercise. Start decreasing the amount of food per feeding by one quarter. If, for example, you feed one cup per feeding to a large Bichon, cut down the portion to ¾ cups per feeding. In addition, eliminate ALL table scraps, treats, wet or canned food, or other little snacks. Increase the exercise level slowly by increasing the distance or time walked. Try to increase pace as well but go slowly to avoid any stress or strain on your

Bichon. Monitor progress every two weeks. Do not decrease the food below the recommended guidelines unless instructed to do so by the vet. If the Bichon is losing weight, continue on your routine. If they are not losing weight, consult your vet and consider moving to a particular weight loss formula for dry food. If you choose this option, be sure to change food slowly to avoid digestive problems. Make sure that your Bichon Frise is not accessing food that you are unaware of. If you have cats or other pets in the house, be sure they are not sneaking their food. Also, make sure that other family members are not giving secret treats and snacks.

Diabetic Bichon Frises

There is somewhat mixed information on whether diet alone can control diabetes in Bichon Frises. Generally, most veterinarians recommend a high fiber, high protein diet, with limited access to fats and carbohydrates used in conjunction with regular insulin therapies. Some specialized foods, usually available through a vet, provide the correct balance to help with blood sugar levels in diabetic dogs. It is very important to stay within feeding guidelines and to carefully monitor your Bichon when they are out of the house to ensure they don't get into other food items.

Diabetic Bichons should not be fed table scraps or treats, as these often contain high levels of carbohydrates, sugars, and fats. Instead, consider making some high protein treats by thinly slicing turkey hotdogs or all-beef hotdogs and microwaving the slices for a minute or two until they are completely dry. These "turkey chips" are a great snack that can be easily stored in a sealed plastic container.

Regular exercise is also important for diabetic Bichons. When exercise, insulin therapy, and high fiber and high protein foods are provided, usually diabetes can be controlled and poses no serious health threat to the Bichon. Uncontrolled or unregulated diabetes can cause death, so immediately contact your vet if you notice rapid weight gain or loss, increasing water consumption, and frequent urination in your pet.

Chapter Five: Raising and Training a Bichon Frise

Training a Bichon Frise is certainly a very meaningful and rewarding experience. This breed is superiorly trainable little pooch that loves to learn a variety of tricks specifically when there is a delectable treat for them involved. Due to this, the enthusiastic and obedient Bichon Frise became the most favorite breed for street and circus performers in the 19th century.

It is valuable to note that Bichons require a lot of kind words and positive reinforcement when undergoing training. Negative attitude and extremely rough discipline will only dishearten the eager to please this breed. A lot of owners of this insightful breed prefer to have their pooches compete in agility and obedience tests.

Crate Training

Crate training your Bichon Frise is an important part of dog ownership. You will want to buy a nice dog crate for your Bichon Frise to train him to use it in positive ways. The crate is a useful tool in keeping your dog calm, as well as training your dog. Plus, he'll love it.

Why Crate Training Your is Important

Dogs are inherently cave dwellers. They love having a den of their own. A dog crate can be a useful tool as well as a calming hideout for your dog. Your home is a great place for your dog to roam around in, but ideally you should provide a crate that he can call his own space.

The crate should be a positive place where your dog can relax. Therefore, the crate is never used for punishment. Don't use it for punishment, you will create a negative association to the crate and make your dog fear the crate. Instead he will search for a hiding place behind the furniture or otherwise in an unsafe place for his natural need for daily retreat.

How to Begin Crate Training

You can begin crate training your dog at any age. When you first get your Bichon Frise, give him a few days to explore your house and get used to his new surroundings. Then begin to introduce him to his new crate.

Start by encouraging your dog to enter the crate. Praise him when he goes in. Then lock the door and leave him in there for an hour at a time. Never leave him in there for more than four hours without a potty break. You can put toys or treats in the crate to help ensure that he feels it is a home atmosphere.

As your Bichon Frise becomes potty trained and learns not to tear up everything in sight, you can then leave the crate door open for him to use it as he pleases. He will probably go in there every now and again to take a nap or to rest for a while by himself, as well as to get away from other more dominating or active dogs, when he's not in the mood to socialize with them. When crate training, be sure to praise him when you see him going into the crate on his own to teach him that the crate is a good thing.

Always give your dog potty breaks. A Bichon Frise puppy needs to go at least every hour. Most older dogs can hold it up to five hours comfortably. Also, be sure to remove soiled items from the crate, especially if your dog releases waste inside it in order that he does not turn it into his miniature porta-potty.

Once your Bichon Frise is fond of his crate, you can start to use it when you are gone. Leave the crate door unlocked once fully trained from bad habits. Let him use it freely. It can help to calm potential separation anxiety that he may suffer while you are away. If you do lock it, be sure not to leave him in there for too long, or adversely turn the dog crate into a punishment tool. If you do this, he will instead learn to not like the crate and soon being to resist going into it. This deprives him of his natural habit and need of it which and while you are gone, he will express as only he knows how to in the form of frustration, with barking, scratching, gnawing, nipping, howling, even whimpering, as well as other naughty things out of anxiety.

Picking the Perfect Crate

Of course, the crate you choose needs to fit your dog. Buy a crate that will match your Bichon Frise's grown size. When fully grown, he should be able to stand up, turn around, and lie down in this crate comfortably. The crate will seem too big when a puppy is little. In such a case simply block off the extra space at the back of the crate. You can use a box or hang a towel to do so. This will help to prevent in-crate-pooping too.

A crate that is enclosed with only slats for your dog to see out of on the sides and the front is ideal for Bichon Frise dogs. He'll want to observe his surroundings. This helps when things become noisy around him because he can see where the sounds come from.

The crate is not an isolation cell. However, you also want to make sure that the crate is not too open. It needs to be an enclosed den where he can have his privacy when needed.

Open metal crates are not enclosed enough, cover it with a thick blanket, leaving narrow spaces on the sides that he can see out of.

Where to Place your Dog Crate

Place the crate close to where you spend the most time together while you are all awake in the house. Put it in a central area, against the wall. The idea is to keep your dog from feeling isolated and away from everything, while owning his own place in it too.

Furnishing the Crate

What you put in the crate is up to you. The crate should be a comfortable place where your dog can hang out as he wants, so be sure to place a pillow or some type of dog bed in it. You can also put toys and treats in the crate.

It's a good idea to put clean water in the crate. To avoid spillage and a mess, get a water bowl that clips onto the crate's door. You can also attach a food bowl if you will be crating your dog for a lengthy period while you are away.

When your dog is left alone, he will miss you no matter how much training he gets, or from whom. A great trick to reduce anxiety is to leave a piece of your unwashed clothing inside with him, such as a sock or shirt. If you want it back in good condition, you'll want to nip nipping and chewing in the bud first.

Positive-Reinforcement Training

One of the most popular training methods for dogs today is positive reinforcement training. This type of training is a version of operant conditioning in which the dog learns to associate an action with a consequence. In this case, the term consequence does not refer to something bad, it is just something that happens as a result of something else. The goal of positive reinforcement training is to encourage your dog to WANT to do what you want him to do.

The basics of positive reinforcement training are simple, you teach the dog that if he follows your commands he will be rewarded. For example, you teach your dog to respond to the word "Sit" by him sitting down. In order to teach him to associate the command with the action, you reward him with a treat each time he sits on command. It generally only takes a few repetitions for dogs to learn to respond to commands because food rewards are highly motivational for most dogs.

The key to successful positive reinforcement-based training sessions is to keep them short and fun. If the dog enjoys the training, he will be more likely to retain what he has learned. It is also important that you make the connection between the command and the desired response very clear to your dog. If he doesn't understand what you want him to do he will become confused. It is also important to pair the reward immediately with the desired response. This helps your dog to make the connection more quickly and it motivates him to repeat the desired behavior.

Punishment-Based Training

Punishment-based training is not as harsh as the word suggests. It is not exactly the opposite of positive reinforcement training, but it is very different. While positive reinforcement training is about encouraging your dog to repeat a desired behavior, punishment-based training is about discouraging your dog from performing an unwanted behavior. The goal of punishment-based training is to teach your dog that a certain action results in a negative consequence and thus the dog will choose not to perform that behavior in the future.

The problem with punishment-based training methods is that it is generally only effective in teaching your dog to stop doing something rather than teaching him to respond to a certain command. It is also important to note that punishment-based training can have a negative impact on your relationship with your dog. Even though your dog may stop performing the unwanted behavior, it may not be because you taught him that the behavior is undesirable. He will likely only associate the behavior with fear and pain (depending on the type of punishment you use).

In addition to learning not to perform the behavior in question, your dog will also learn to be fearful of you. If you know anything about dog behavior, you may already know that, in most cases, aggression is born of fear. Even the most even-tempered dog can become aggressive if he is afraid. If you use punishment-based training methods you not only risk teaching your dog to fear you, but there is also the possibility that he will become aggressive with you at some point in the future.

Note: I would like to point out here, that if you adopt this style of training, you should NEVER, under any circumstances hit your dog. It is not only cruel, but an unnecessary action on your part. If you are ever having recurring behavioral issues with your dog, you should either seek an alternative approach or in extreme cases, seek the help of a professional dog trainer.

Clicker Training

Clicker training is a very effective way to get into your dog's head and align his subconscious to act instinctively on command once a command is trained with it. The essence of clicker training is to use a dog clicker device that makes a clicking sound to teach your dog an association between the sound of the click, a command, and a reward if he follows the command. Dogs learn fast through conditioning, and the clicker really helps cement this conditioning. '

Things to Consider

The first thing to understand is that the clicker is a teaching device. It is not something that you will always need to use. Once your dog learns to follow your commands, you can put the clicker away. You will not need to carry it on your person at all times during the entire course of your dog ownership. Unless you yourself enjoy the sound of a snappy clicker while on solo walks. To each their own.

The second thing to realize is that treats are not the only reward you can offer. They are very effective, especially when training your Bichon Frise initially. However, once he gets your commands down, you can more often reward his good behavior with love and praise, a toy, and only the occasional treat. Mix it up to keep him guessing and looking forward to what he might get if he obeys you.

Finally, dog treats don't need to be calorie-laden. Give your dog small things, like a tiny piece of jerky or a kernel of corn, or any number of brand name healthy and fortified doggie treats on the market. Here's why, because they are less than bite sized treats, although you treat him often enough, smaller treats will not tire him out, make him lazy or gain weight. Plus, they are easy to carry in your pocket, or you can purchase a dog treat pouch for a nominal price at amazon, or your local pet shop when on a walk with your dog. Keep these treats concealed. For instance, you are trying to teach your dog to sit, so you tell him the sit command. When he does it, you then produce the toy or treat hiding in your pocket and let him have it.

A good exercise is to stop your Bichon Frise during play and give him a command. Take his toy away and hold onto it.

Use a command. When he does it, click and then give him the toy back.

How the Clicker Works

The clicker works using what's known in training your dog as shaping. Shaping is where you use progressive steps to teach your dog a desired command. You basically shape his mind by rewarding him each time that he performs a step as you desire. As well you will add more time to hold the command in each successive shaping. Eventually, your pup will learn to associate the clicking noise with a reward. He will learn that by doing something you ask, he will hear a click, and then he will get a reward. Eventually, the conditioning will become so strong that he will stop needing the clicker or the treat. He will just do what you command. *"Now, That's a Good Boy!"*

You may wonder why a clicker is better than saying "Good" or some other verbal cue. This is because the clicker is a unique sound that your dog cannot mistake for anything else. The human voice can vary in tone and sound at different times, and some commands sound alike in many of our English words. But the click never varies in volume or sound. It is consistent. And we love consistency in training your Bichon Frise.

How to Perform Clicker Training

Buy a clicker from amazon.com or your local pet supply store. Then use it whenever you teach your dog a new command, behavior or trick. Use a click when he gets the command right. Then follow it up with a reward.

Consistency is key. You want to use the clicker at the exact moment your dog does what you command. You can use it when he obeys a command you give, or when he does something on his own. Use your clicker during training until your dog has listening to you perfected.

Start by teaching your pup a command. When teaching him to stay, only click and reward when he is completely still. When teaching him to sit, you may need to push his body into a sitting position. Once he is sitting down, you click and reward. This teaches him exactly what behavior is desired when you make a command or give him a cue.

You can also teach him to associate responding to a certain stimulus with a desired behavior. For instance, staying quiet when the mailman arrives is something that you can teach him to do with the clicker. Click and reward him when he does not bark at the mailman.

Never offer a click or a reward when your Bichon Frise does not do the desired action. Doing this will only confuse him. You want to stay consistent. Teach him to only expect clicks and rewards when he does what you want.

If your dog is not responding to clicker training, then consider that you are doing something wrong. Maybe you are confusing him. Try working on teaching him the command or cue more. Read this again. Be clearer, more direct about it and eliminate distractions.

Maybe you are offering too many treats, so he is preoccupied with food and not listening to you. In this case, pause for a while. Twenty minutes or so, then return to training. Mix it up a bit and offer other rewards besides treats. On the other hand, maybe the reward you offer is not cutting it for him. I suggest you don't use sauerkraut, that's for a different type of dog you may find on the streets of New York.

Is he nipping and spitting, or gobbling them down as if each treat is the only one left in the dog world? Perhaps your Bichon Frise does not view it as worth the effort. In such a case, change the reward to something that he prefers. Switch out an unpopular toy with his favorite one or find treats that he really likes.

Maybe you have only trained your dog at home. Now that you are out in public, he thinks the context is different. Work on graduating to new and different environments to get him to understand that commands or cues are the same no matter where he is.

Clicker training can come with some trial and error. Consider this a long-term partnership with your special buddy. Gauge what you do and how you do it based on his responses. Keep what works, dump what doesn't and replace it with what does. Command, Click, Treat.

Teach your Bichon Frise bathroom schedule

Always an eye on him and spot signs of his desire to urinate or defecate- then bring him out. Teach him that outside is the right place to do his business, not inside the crate. When you are done housebreaking, allow him to exercise for few minutes before taking him back to the crate. Praise him when he goes to the specified area to urinate or defecate. Allow him to move around. Plan an outing or a walk when you know he is in the right state of mind.

Try paper training

Most Bichon are particularly stubborn about housebreaking. If you keep on having issues with him going outside, then try paper training. Paper training simply means training your Bichon that he can urinate or defecate inside only on one condition- that he uses pads, newspapers or other available absorbent materials in your house.

Veterinary doctors and expert breeders say that you should use positive reinforcement while training your

Bichon. Praise him anytime he uses the right materials indoors and correct him if he does not. Don't scold or get hysterical or resort to yelling, such actions will frighten the dog or make him to get frustrated. Male Bichons finds it difficult to get along with paper training than females.

Teach them not to bite

Bichons remains a friendly breed. They bite easily, but this biting is normally a non-aggressive form of play. But most of them don't know that biting is painful to humans, so it is your duty to train them on this, especially if you have children in your family or neighborhood.

Bichons bite for several reasons- either as an attempt to play or assert an authority. They will get bored and stop if their biting is not getting a positive response from people.

Always supervise your children's interaction with Bichon. Don't allow your children to interrupt them while they are sleeping, eating, drinking water or playing with toys. Your Bichon might bite if they become territorial.

If you discover any sign of biting from your Bichon, correct him immediately with a stern 'No'. Teach him that biting is good as long as he does it to his snacks or toys, not people. Biting to humans is not encouraged for any reason.

Practice good leash manners

Bichons remains excellent walking companions to their owners. Teach them the basics of leash training. Ensure they are comfortable and familiar with his collar. Keep teaching and supervising him until he gets used to wearing the collar.

Gradually introduce him to it, let him sniff and familiarize himself with it. Praise him if he is happy walking by your side. Taking a 15 to 20 minutes of walk daily around your neighborhood, will make him to adapt or familiarize himself with walking on a leash.

Beware of other dog syndrome

Make sure your Bichon feels confident, safe and happy when they are near larger dogs. Teach him never to seem nervous in the presence of other dogs, praise him, give him treats and talk to him calmly if he stays calm. Every act of aggression, barking or nipping should never go unchecked.

Teach your Bichon how to sit and lie down

Teaching your Bichon to sit and lie down are foundational commands that you need to start teaching your dogs. Keep repeating these commands 10 to 15 times daily until your dogs learn the principles of sitting and lying down. You can use treat to lure him into sitting or lying down.

Teach your Bichon to come

The word 'come' is a simple command that most dogs learns easily. Knowing when to come will prevent your dogs from accidents in certain situations. Praise them or give them toys they like when they come to you upon hearing the command 'come'.

Get involved in other training opportunities

There are many ways to train your dogs to develop elaborate skills- once they know the importance of sitting, lying down and coming. You can enroll them in a dog training class, where they will be coached by a professional trainer. Training remains a veritable way of socializing your Bichon.

With proper training, your Bichon will learn how to behave in the presence of other pets. Bichons are perfect hospital and/or therapy dogs. They have naturally friendly personality and love to stay with people.

Mentally Stimulating Activities for Bichons

It is important it is to keep your Bichon Frise active and busy for both his physical and mental health. But physical activity is not all that your dog needs to be healthy and happy. Bichon Frises also need to keep their minds busy, or they can get bored and turn to bored-replacement activities like barking, chewing, and digging. You can prevent a lot of bad behaviors by providing your dog with mentally stimulating activities, like the following:

- Retrieval games. Add challenges by hiding toys or throwing them into hard-to-access places so that your dog must puzzle out how to get the toy.

- Obstacle courses. Turn your home, garage, or back yard into an obstacle course and make your dog overcome it by rewarding dog treats when accomplishing completion.

- A Kong full of peanut butter. He can spend hours trying to lick the peanut butter out. An occupied dog is a happy dog.

- Flyball. This will keep him active physically and mentally.

- Socialization and play with other dogs. He will invent his own games and feel very stimulated in the company of other dogs. Take him to the dog park or enroll him in puppy classes where he can play with other dogs.

- Herding livestock or Triebball. Triebball uses balls that mimic herd animals that dogs must manage.

- Tracking. Hide an object in the woods or a field and let your dog find it with his natural scent abilities.

- Herding trials or tests. These will let your Bichon Frise use his natural herding ability.

- Agility games. Set up an agility course in your yard and teach your dog obedience and tricks as you teach him to navigate the equipment.

Separation Anxiety

Separation anxiety (SA) in dogs is defined as a condition in which a dog exhibits distress and behavioral problems whenever it is separated from its handler. Generally, this behavior will surface within thirty minutes of the separation from the dog's handler.

Separation anxiety can occur not only within puppies, but it can also manifest in adult dogs. With puppies, anxiety related behaviors usually begin when they are first removed from their littermates and mother. The reasons for anxiety behaviors in adult dogs can vary, though they can also be related to the original separation from its family when they were a puppy. Other events that can be responsible for the presence of anxiety in an animal can be related to a traumatic event, such as some type of previous physical injury, mistreatment, and abandonment, all of which can be causes for anxiety related behaviors when separated from its owner.

It must be taken into consideration that some of the normal processes of aging in an animal, such as hearing and sight loss can also contribute to, or exacerbate the potential for higher levels of anxiety. It is important to be able to recognize healthy and abnormal behaviors. By recognizing the signs and symptoms of abnormal behaviors, then you can be prepared to intervene with proactive measures to reduce the negative effects.

Several of the normal behaviors that may occur for those puppies who have recently arrived into a new home can manifest in many ways. Ongoing whining, a constant want for touch or affection, and their need to shadow you wherever you go are some of the most common signs of separation anxiety. Since the puppy is experiencing a variety of new sensations in an unfamiliar environment these behaviors are normal.

The instinct to survive, will motivate a puppy to remain near to their caretaker, thus sticking close to their new provider should be a normal and expected behavior. Often, if a puppy is left alone, he or she will whine, bark, or even howl to express their discomfort from being alone. Your dog's individual personality will dictate how long these behaviors last during your absence. It is common that your dog will find something to pacify itself in this alone time, such as gnawing upon one of his chewy toys. It is usual for these behaviors to cease after a short time, and should not be an ongoing, day and night occurrence that last regularly over thirty minutes. Yes, these sounds can be distressing to listen to, but remember that they are normal expressions while they learn to adapt to their new environment. Do not be alarmed because this is just a phase in their development, and it will soon pass.

Allowing your new puppy to remain alone for periods of time, is a necessary component of his socialization training which allows him to experience time alone and gradual exposure to mechanical noises, other humans, animals, and the exciting world of his new environment. As said prior, it is important to keep in mind that sometimes the upsetting behaviors he displays are normal but they will subside over time. Positive training in combination with consistent socialization will empower your puppy to overcome these anxieties and gain the self-confidence to develop into a well-adjusted adult dog. Training sessions work as an important component for building self-confidence and a puppy's character, but in itself is not a cure for separation anxiety.

Deeper Separation Anxiety

Identifying a puppy or adult dog that is experiencing a deeper, chronic anxiety can be detected by an awareness that his separation behaviors are heightened and frequently displayed. Clinically, this would be diagnosed by a veterinarian as a chronic, pathological form of separation anxiety, and may need psychological or medical intervention. For example, extended durations of whining, barking, or crying lasting thirty minutes to an hour or more is an indication of a greater problem. In extreme cases, this heightened behavior might be intermixed with a more frantic barking, and perhaps howling or whining that may continue until your puppy becomes completely exhausted from his expressions of stress.

Other signs of anxiety can appear in an inability to remain calm or still, acting out by pacing rapidly, spinning in place, or jumping up and down sometimes in a hysterical and frantic manner. While being contained in his crate or gated area, he might tear excessively at the interior, his blankets, flooring, toys, or anything else he can get his little razor teeth, or tiny paws into. This behavior should be recognized not as a regular chewing behavior that well-adjusted dogs' display, but instead intentional destructive behavior, physically acting out his anxiety and deep-rooted distress.

Signs of stress also can manifest in the form of drooling, continuous panting, and frequent yawning. Loss of bladder and bowel control can lead to frequent accidents, and diarrhea and loose stools are common when an animal is stressed. Obsessive-compulsive behaviors such as excessive gnawing, licking or chewing upon his own body, including the feet need to be treated by a veterinarian.

If your dog is displaying signs of depression, anxiety, or excessive excitement each time you prepare to leave, or if his greetings are hysterical and unrestrained, and he is following you from room to room, these are indicators of separation anxiety, and need immediate attention.

If you have determined that your puppy is suffering from Separation Anxiety by his signs and symptoms, then you have to begin the important journey of teaching your puppy that not everything is bad nor has a potential for lasting trauma or discomfort. Instead, teach him that his new environment and the world is a nurturing place, not something to be feared, and that if you are not around, his world will not end. Treating your puppy's issues will take some time and patience and perhaps some assistance from professionals who are trained in these animal behaviors.

Preventing Separation Anxiety from developing is the best plan to undertake, first beginning in puppyhood, and then following up with your adult dog who perhaps exhibits the symptoms. Following these simple steps below should keep your puppy or full-grown dog from developing or displaying any severe behaviors and reduce the symptoms of separation anxiety.

Prevention of Separation Anxiety

- Your new pup is the cutest fur-ball of joy that you have ever seen, right. Heck, you picked him out of the litter and brought him home to become a member of your family. Although the desire to hold, coddle, cuddle, and fondle our pets whenever possible, may be a deep part of our human nature, it is during these times of innate urges to display a little restraint.

As difficult as I know it can be, refrain from carrying him around with you wherever you go and limit your compulsion to shower him with constant, syrupy affection. These actions, though pleasing to the both of you, can serve as the catalyst for the onset of separation anxiety. These actions create a dependency for that loving warmth that you lavish on him. If not nipped in the bud early on, this will be more difficult to curb in the future.

- Whether awake or asleep, give your little pup some space of his own. A little distance and autonomy goes a long way to help create healthy independence. Remember as you are doing this, it is neither cruel nor neglect, but in actuality this distance constitutes an essential element of the proactive measures that will help him feel secure when he is on his own.

What you want to avoid is creating a puppy that never wants to leave your side, and is in constant fear of being away from the safety, comfort and attention that you may continually bestow upon him. Although well intended, the attention that you may continually shower on him will result in having a "shadow" dog, which will neither benefit you, nor will it be healthy for him. Give him some space throughout your days together, and resist the craving to keep him with you everywhere you go.

- Begin leaving your puppy alone from the first day that you bring him home. Whether contained in his crate or restricted to his gated area, I advise that keep you keep him out of eyesight. Start the periods of separation with short durations of about 2-4 minutes each. As he begins to cope with this initial interval without freaking out and becoming agitated, then gradually, increase the extent of time that he is left alone. Leaving your pup alone should be done at least two or three times per day. During this time, it is essential to ignore any of his whimpering, whining, or any other form of agitation he may express. Do not confuse this exercise with neglect.

- *How to act when leaving your puppy alone.* Don't make a big deal of it when you are leaving, especially by showing exaggerated or disproportionate emotions that may in fact display your own human separation anxiety. This is dangerously contagious to our canine friends.

Before you depart, simply make sure he is confined in an area that is of a comfortable temperature, that he has plenty of chew-toys, and fresh water. Oh! In addition, please don't forget to let the little guy relieve himself before you take off.

In the moment of your departure, use a positive tone of voice and a brief expression of farewell, using a simple phrase, such as "Goodbye, be back soon," will suffice. Stay clear of sappy, long and drawn out emotional partings. If you make a dramatic sendoff, this may become the creation of fear and concern, setting into motion a situation that may promote an elevation in the level of anxiety he will experience as you leave, thus resulting in all of the negative behaviors associated with SA.

- *Act similar upon returning.* Upon returning home, do not immediately make eye contact with your pup, or run to him as though it has been days since you have seen each other. If you have been gone for over an hour, then it is fine to go pick him up and say hello, immediately followed by a relief break. When he is finished with his business, place him back into his puppy area and return to your business. If you have only been away for a few minutes, a casual hello or quick pet will suffice, and it is not necessary to immediately make eye contact with him, or even acknowledge his existence.

- As part of supporting good puppy health and maintaining your alpha dominance, it is important to set a consistent schedule for feeding, playing, training, and relieving times by creating a routine of the activities for daily living.
- *Human advice.* Control your temper; he cannot help his crying out for attention. If your puppy is getting upset and simply driving you crazy with his whimpering, crying, barking, or howling, remember to keep your alpha composure by being even-tempered, firm, fair, and consistent in your actions. Keep in mind that *you* are in charge and it is *you* that dictates the rules and schedules, *not your darling, adorable little sidekick.*

Troubleshooting Separation Anxiety

If you have a puppy or an adult dog that is displaying what appears to be clinical symptoms of moderate to severe separation anxiety, it is likely that professional interventions need to be sought out, followed by more advanced and focused training methods. Even though S.A. occurs in a very small percentage of domestic dogs, a dog with separation anxiety will nonetheless make life difficult for you and your family. If left untreated, this can lead to health complications and ongoing behavioral problems.

If your puppy or adult dog has a range of negative behaviors ranging from excessive destruction of property, fearfulness, barking, whimpering, whining, or anxiousness, then below are some techniques that can be used to relieve some of the symptoms. If your dog is suffering from some these behaviors, it is possible that with your proactive measures and concerted efforts your dog will be capable of displaying calmer mannerisms and an improved mental health. Reducing the effects SA is having upon your puppy will also greatly improve your mental health status.

Minor symptoms of nervousness can be handled with some simple dog training techniques.

- Remove boredom from your puppy's life. Supply plenty of chew-toys, at least 30- minutes of daily vigorous exercise (age appropriate), one to two daily training sessions of obedience commands, and socialization sessions.
- Exercise in the form of a brisk walk or short game of fetch before your planned absence can burn away any surplus energy reserves that if not expended can serve to trigger further anxiousness during your absence.
- While you are gone, it can be soothing to leave a low volume radio or television on to distract or comfort him. Prior to doing this, test it out to see if it is actually soothing rather than agitating your puppy.
- Occupy alone time with stuffed chew-toys. These toys can be stuffed in such a way that make it a time-consuming project for him to extract the food, thus keeping him distracted for long periods of time. The nice thing about these chew toys is that

it is impossible to bark, whine, or cry while chewing them.

Moderate symptoms will appear as more severe than the features of minor nervousness, and needs to be tackled with more intensive behavioral modification techniques that will require daily practice through focused dog training that can take weeks or months to solve the issue.

- First, increase the daily exercise routine keeping within the recommended limits of your puppy's breed. Take care to make sure your little pup does not over-heat, and if he is an extra-large breed be careful that he is not jumping or doing anything that may injure his growing bones.

Begin multiple daily rigorous exercise regimens that utilize games, brisk walks, and if possible, fit in 2-3 outings of fetch games. If your dog refuses to play fetch, then substitute some other type of play or exercise that will increase his heart rate and use up some of his energy reserves. Try for a minimum of two 30-minute activity-based periods per day.

- Two daily short 10-minute training sessions of the basic commands, followed by teaching down-stay or sit-stay is advised. The commands of sit-stay and down-stay are great in creating confidence in your dog so that he can be left alone by teaching him to accept distance between the two of you in different places, and at different times.

- Another great option is that when your puppy is old enough, and had at least his first round of shots, is to enroll him into a puppy kindergarten class. This will increase his socialization skills, and build confidence under the guidance of a trained professional. These classes also instruct humans on how to train and interact with their puppies.

- If you have a dog that we refer to as a "Shadow dog," which means a dog that refuses to leave your side, then it is essential that you work on gradually increasing the space between the two of you. This is easy to do by using his crate or gated area as his isolation areas, and progressively increasing the duration that you are separated. Beginning with short durations of time apart or when you notice a pause in his fretting is the time you should free him from his confines. When you free him from his confines, be sure not to make a big deal about it, act as if it is just a normal daily routine. Take special care and make appropriate adjustments if your dog is still displaying destructive behaviors or becoming extremely agitated in his isolation areas, especially in his crate. If this is the case, do not use his crate for this particular training. We want our puppies to love their crates and find them a safe haven.

Desensitizing your puppy to your absence is another way to help him through the miseries of his separation anxiety. Sometimes the simplest action, such as grabbing your jacket, bag or the sounds of keys clanging can be a stimulus for your puppy begin to feel anxious in anticipation of your absence.

- To begin to desensitize your puppy to your departures, start by acting out the preparations to leave, but not actually leaving the house. Go through the motions, such as grabbing your house keys, or briefcase, but instead of leaving, just walk around the house for a couple of minutes carrying your things. After doing that, put your things away. Practice this three to five times a day until your dog ceases showing signs of agitation or nervousness during your *faux departure* preparations. The success of this training varies in duration from dog to dog. Depending upon your dog and his predisposition, this training could take a day, a couple of days, a week, or even longer.

- The next step is to repeat the step above, but now leave the premises. Begin by leaving for only a few seconds and then returning indoors. During this training, gradually increase the time that you wait outside of your house before returning inside. The key here is never to make a big deal of leaving or coming home, just act as if it is an event not worthy of attention or emotion. Simply grab your things and leave. Continue this training until your dog becomes less and less disturbed by this whole affair of you coming and going.

- Upon returning home after a lengthy leave, walk inside and immediately tend to your normal life, ignoring your dog for at least five to ten minutes. After this duration, or when you are ready to show attention and affection, then go to your dog and give him the love he deserves.

How to lessen your dog's symptoms when you are going to leave:

1. Take your pup for a quick fast-paced walk or vigorous exercise session.
2. Turn on the radio or television to lessen the loneliness. If this has proved to be soothing and not agitating.
3. Leave plenty of toys to keep him busy.
4. When you leave, leave quickly without emotional outpourings towards your dog.

Extra Helpings for Separation Anxiety Training

1. Hire a pet sitter or dog walker to visit at least once during the day.
2. Ask your neighbors how your dog is acting while you are away.
3. Once or twice a week, drop your dog at a doggie day-care facility.
4. If the dog training tips within this guide do not seem to work for you, solicit outside help from a professional trainer and speak with your veterinarian.

5. As a last resort, after trying all of the suggestions above, there are medications available to help calm your dog. I recommend that this is a temporary solution, as a part of a holistic therapy, while you continue to shape and change your dog's behavior using the methods and techniques described. If choose to use medication, research for the safest natural product on the market, or rely on the advice of your dog's vet.

6. Avoid leaving your dog crated for long periods.

7. Avoid punishments for SA related accidents or incidents. Remember that because of the deep-seated nature of his problem, a dog with SA is not in control of himself. For example, as demonstrated by soiling issues related to his anxieties.

The goal and final outcome of this training is to have a healthy, happy, well-adjusted dog that can handle any situation that comes his way. As previously mentioned, prevention of Separation Anxiety can afford you the peace of mind knowing that you will not have to go through this rigorous training, as well as never having to deal with the aggravation of incessant whimpering, barking, gnawing, tearing, and other doggie anxiety actions that will negatively affect you, your family, visiting friends and your neighbors. Some statistics indicate that only about 10-15% of the population of domestic dogs become afflicted with some degree of separation anxiety.

Giving your Bichon Frise a Treat

So, you're training your Bichon Frise and he is doing well, of course, you're thinking of giving him a treat. But you want to make sure you're giving him the right kind of treats. Treats are easy. As long as you stay away from the things that aren't good for dogs; Avocado, onions and garlic, in any form, coffee, tea or caffeine, grapes, raisins, macadamia nuts, peaches, plums, pits, persimmons or chocolate, whiskey soda, to name a few.

You can make a treat from many foods. Treats should be small, corn nut sized, and easy to grab from a pocket or container. When you are outdoors and there are many distractions, treats should be better quality, cubes of cheese, dried meat, and such. Make sure you mix them up, Nothing is worse for treat training than your dog turning his nose up at a treat because he has had it too often.

Here are some treat ideas:

- Cubed meats
- Shredded cheese
- Cream cheese, peanut butter, or easy cheese. Give your dog a lick for every proper behavior.
- Cereal, Cheerios is good, no milk, no bowl, and no spoon, just the goods
- Kibble (dry foods). Put some in a paper bag and smell it up with some bacon or other meat.
- Beef Jerky
- Carrot or apple pieces
- Meat baby food, you know those little suspect sausage things. You would cry too c'mon now.

- Commercial dog treats. Careful here, there are tons of them on the market. Look for those that do not have preservatives, by products, or artificial colors.
- Ice cube. Not the rapper, the frozen water treats. Yup, your dog will love crunching these up.

Chapter Six: Grooming Your Bichon Frise

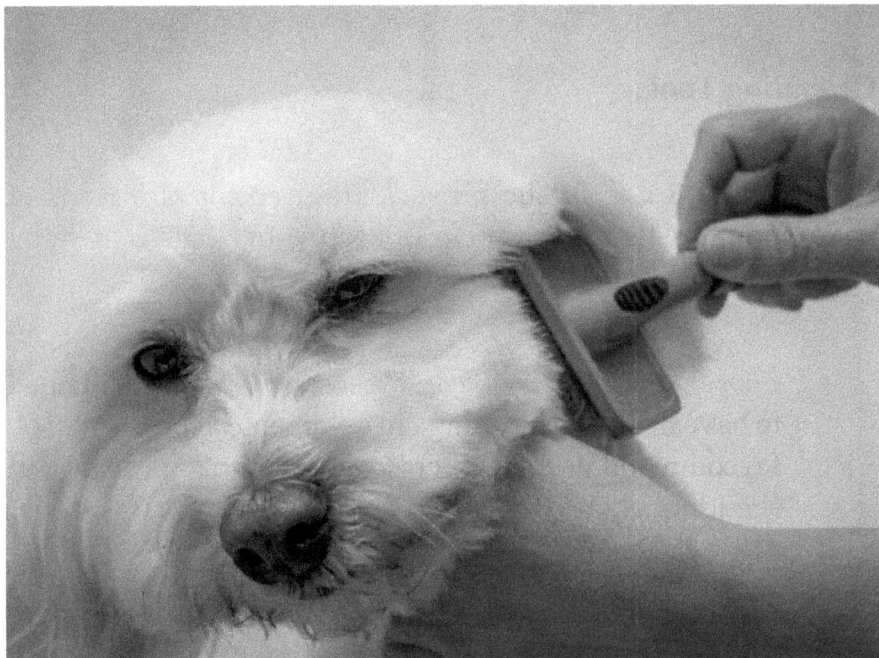

Grooming

Grooming your Bichon Frise is very important. Not only does grooming help to control shedding but it also helps to ensure that your dog's coat and skin remain healthy. In this part, you will learn the basics about grooming your Bichon Frise including tips for cleaning your dog's ears and trimming his nails. Please be aware that this is the one aspect of the Bichon Frise that is relatively demanding and time consuming. It is also very important that regular grooming is applied. Grooming doesn't have to take over your life, it depends on whether you want a show dog look or a pet trim. Either way, daily brushing is highly recommended.

Grooming Tools

- *Bristle Brush:* Bristle brushes are used for all breeds of dog. Bristle brushes help to keep your dog's coat shiny and free from dirt.

- *Clippers and Shedding Blade:* Most species of dog will need to have their coats trimmed in summer to keep them cool. I recommend using clippers for dogs with long coats and shedding blades for short hair dogs.

- *De-Matting Rake:* De-matting rakes have long wire prongs. These prongs are great for removing matts from long coats. It is important to use this tool gently to avoid causing your dog discomfort.

- *Rubber Brush:* Rubber brushes are great for removing dead hair. They create a massaging effect which many dogs enjoy.

- *Slicker Brush:* Slicker brushes are used to remove tangles and dead hair. They have rows of bent wire pins. They should only be used on dogs with long or thick hair.

- *Nail Clippers:* Nail clippers should be scissor shaped to allow for best control. It is important to purchase sharp nail clippers and to always have a spare set (in case one set become blunt).

- *Nail File:* Nail files are used to file the end of your dog's toe nail after it has been clipped. It is important to purchase a high-quality nail file as it will allow the filing process to be completed much quicker.

Bathing

If you have to wash mud from their legs, feet or coat, please do this with warm water, but no shampoo. You can then either towel dry and or use a hair drier to ensure your dog does not get chilled.

Avoid bathing your dog on a regular basis as this can strip the skin and coat of natural healthy oils. Remember that your Bichon Frise's skin has a pH of around 7.5, while humans have a pH of 5.5. That said, never use human shampoo on your Bichon Frise. This will lead to scaling and skin irritation. There are numerous dog shampoos available for various canine skin problems. It is also advisable to use a good conditioner. Some groomers will also recommend adding a T spoon of baby oil to the conditioner. This helps to to stop the coat and skin from drying out, which is obviously important for Bichon's due to regular bathing.

Don't forget that your dog relies on natural oils to keep the skin soft, healthy and free from drying out. The oil also has the benefit of protecting the coat and retaining its water resistance. It is tempting to consider how grubby and uncomfortable us humans feel when we don't bathe regularly. However, you cannot take that same viewpoint where your dog is concerned.

To bathe your Bichon Frise at home follow the steps outlined below:

1. Give your Bichon Frise a good brushing, as above, before you bathe him to get rid of accumulated loose hair.

2. Fill your bathtub with a few inches of lukewarm water. You may also want to put down a bath mat so your dog doesn't slip in the tub.

3. Place your Bichon Frise in the tub and wet down his fur with a handheld hose or by pouring water over him. Because the Bichon Frise's coat is relatively long, you may need to use your hands to work the water all the way down to his skin.

4. Avoid getting your Bichon Frise's eyes and ears wet when you bathe him. Wet ears are a breeding ground for bacteria that could cause an ear infection.

5. Apply a small amount of mild dog-friendly shampoo to your Bichon Frise's back and gently

work it into a lather along his neck, back, chest and legs.

6. Rinse the soap thoroughly out of your Bichon Frise's coat and use a damp washcloth to clean his face.

7. Use a large fluffy towel to towel-dry your Bichon Frise, getting as much water out of his coat as possible.

You can bathe your Bichon Frise if he gets dirty, but you should avoid bathing him when it is not necessary. Again, over-bathing a dog can dry out his skin and lead to skin problems. In some cases, you may be able to brush dried dirt and debris out of your Bichon Frise's coat instead of bathing him.

a) Blow Drying

You will no doubt have to blow dry the coat after their bath. If you use your own hair dryer, be careful that this is not at its highest hot setting. It is advisable to brush the coat as you blow dry and proceed as follows:

1. You will use the bristle/pin brush first, giving the coat a good brush. The slicker will pull the coat much more initially, so you should use the slicker after the bristle/pin brushing. You then do exactly the same with the slicker brush to get a more pronounced 'powder puff/boufant' look. As you brush, go with the lay of the coat firstly to loosen the hair, then against the lay to obtain the powder

puff look. Concentrate on small sections and work systematically from the tail. You should continuously brush as you blow dry. Please be careful not to pull the coat as you brush. A professional groomer will have a hair dryer on a stand, therefore leaving both hands free. One hand will brush the coat, whilst the other will hold the coat taut in the opposite direction to brushing, and so avoid pulling the skin. Without the hairdryer on a stand, I have to say, the best alternative method is for you have an assistant help you.

2. Now use the same technique on the legs

3. Next brush and blow dry the body

4. Lastly brush and blow the head and ears.

If you would prefer to see this whole process on video, please search [blow drying a bichon] on YouTube. Please note that the whole blow-drying process is likely to take between 25 and 30 minutes. Once you have brushed and blow dried, you are ready to trim.

b) Hair Trimming

When trimming your Bichon, you can do a simple pet trim using a combination of electric clippers and scissors. Electric clippers do provide an easy way to get a relatively uniform look as you simply follow the contours of your dog's legs and body. The disadvantage, is that you are generally limited to the length you can cut. Many professional groomers prefer to trim free hand with scissors as you generally get a fuller look. It is entirely up to you which method you adopt.

You are basically aiming for a rounded look that leaves approximately 1 to 2 inches of hair all round, but obviously this will be closer if clippers are used.

For a trim using scissors, please proceed as follows:

1. Once your dog is properly blow dried, you will need to thoroughly comb the coat. The key here is to comb the hair up away from the lay of the coat as opposed to combing it flat.

2. If the ears are overly thick and fluffy it may be necessary to thin the hair with a pair of thinning scissors. When trimming the flap of the ear itself be very careful that you can see the skin of the ear, as you obviously want to avoid accidentally cutting the ear.

3. Trim excess hair from under the feet, again be very careful not to cut the skin.

4. Trim the hair around the anus in the same manner

5. The tail hair should be left relatively long, so only trim a small amount from the length.

6. The rear needs to have a rounded look with the legs cylindrical. It is advisable when trimming the legs and body to keep the scissors parallel to the standing surface or parallel to the dog's body.

7. Now trim the body hair starting at the top and moving down and underneath. When trimming underneath, it may be necessary to get someone to hold your dog in a standing upright position, so you can easily trim the hair. Again, aim for a consistent look that retains the contours but also has the puffed outlook.

8. The front should look straighter less rounded than the rear, but to still retain the cylindrical look.

9. Be careful when trimming around the eyes. You firstly comb the hair forward over the eyes and then trimmed back so the top of the eyes are showing. Any hair around the eyes should be carefully trimmed.

10. Comb the hair along the bridge of the nose towards the tip of the nose. Comb the hair of the muzzle downwards and trim any excess.

11. The beard should be trimmed in line with the ends of the ears.

That is a very brief step by step trimming guideline. Once again, if you are unsure, always get a professional groomer to guide you in the first instance.

c) Dealing with Eye Stains

Dogs with light-colored fur like the Bichon Frise tend to develop discolored stains in the corners of their eyes. This is common and generally not a problem unless the discharge is yellow or green and if it has an unpleasant odor. These may be signs of infection. If you suspect that your Bichon Frise has an eye infection you should take him to the vet immediately. Otherwise, follow the steps below to clean away eye stains:

1. Mix one-part hydrogen peroxide with 10 parts fresh water in a small container.

2. Dip a clean cotton swab into the solution and rub it gently into the fur around your dog's eyes to remove stains. Be very careful not to get any of the solution into your dog's eyes.

3. Use a clean cloth or cotton ball to dry the area after you have removed the stains.

4. Add one teaspoon of distilled white vinegar or apple cider vinegar to your dog's drinking water. This will change the pH of the water and help to prevent bacterial growth that leads to staining.

5. Keep the fur around your dog's eyes trimmed short. If the hair gets into your dog's eyes it could cause irritation leading to excessive tearing.

In most cases, tear staining in Bichon Frises is not a serious problem. It can affect the way your dog looks but it may not be the result of a medical problem. If your dog's tearing becomes excessive or recurrent, take your dog to the vet to identify and treat the underlying cause.

Trimming the Nails

Trimming your Bichon Frise's nails can be challenging because you need to be very careful. A dog's nail contains a quick; the vessel that brings blood to the nail. If you cut the nail too short you will cut the quick. This not only causes your dog pain, but it can bleed profusely as well. When you trim your Bichon Frise's nails you should only cut the very tip to remove the point. Depending on what color your dog's nails are, you may be able to see the quick and use it as a trimming guide.

It is generally recommended that you trim your Bichon Frise's nails every two weeks. If you do it this often then you will only need to clip the slightest amount off the nail each time. This will reduce the risk of cutting the quick. Before you trim your Bichon Frise's nails for the first time you should consider having a veterinarian or a professional groomer show you how. You also need to be sure you are using real dog nail clippers for the job. Please also be aware that you shouldn't attempt to clip your dog's nails routinely every two weeks, just for the sake of it, as he may not need it. You should notice that if your dog walks on pavements or your concrete yard, he will to a certain extent be filing them down anyway.

Cleaning the Ears

Because the Bichon Frise's ears hang down over the sides of his head there is an increased risk of ear infections. Drop ears, results in air and moisture being trapped under the flap of the ear, making it a breeding ground for bacteria. Your dog's risk for ear infection increases significantly if you get the ears wet, such as during a bath.

Cleaning your dog's ears is not difficult, but you do need the right supplies. Gear up with a bottle of dog-friendly ear cleaning solution and a few clean cotton balls. Gently lift your dog's ear and squeeze a few drops of the cleaning solution into the ear canal. Rub the base of your dog's ear with your fingers to spread the solution then use the cotton balls to wipe it away. Be careful not to put your fingers or the cotton ball too far into your dog's ear or you could damage his ear drum. The frequency with which you clean your Bichon Frise's ears will vary, but you should aim for once every week or two.

Cleaning your dog's ears is not difficult, but you do need the right supplies. Gear up with a bottle of dog-friendly ear cleaning solution, preferably recommended by your vet, and a few clean cotton balls.

1. Gently hold your dog's ear and squeeze a few drops of the cleaning solution into the ear canal.

2. Massage the ear canal, around the base of the dog's ear, to spread the solution then use the cotton balls to wipe it away.

3. Be careful not to put your fingers or the cotton ball too far into your dog's ear or you could damage his ear drum.

Please also avoid cleaning with cotton buds as again they could cause internal damage. The frequency with which you clean your Bichon Frise's ears will vary but you should aim for once every week or two.

Brushing the teeth

The idea of brushing your dog's teeth may sound strange but dental health is just as important for your dog as it is for you. In fact, periodontitis (gum disease) is five times more common in dogs than in humans. Gum disease is incredibly serious but it often goes unnoticed by pet parents, especially since many people think that dogs are supposed to have bad breath. Bad breath, or halitosis, is one of the most common signs of gum disease and could be indicative of a tooth abscess. Once again, please note that dogs regularly chewing on suitable raw meaty bones have relatively odorless breath. If you suspect an abscess, or anything un-toward, seek a veterinary examination as soon as possible.

To brush your Bichon Frise's teeth, follow the steps below:

- Select a soft-bristle toothbrush to use. Most pet stores stock special toothbrushes for dogs.

- Choose a toothpaste that is specifically made for dogs, never human tooth paste. They come in a variety of flavors, so select one your Bichon Frise will like. He will probably like them all. Again, never use the tooth paste you use. These contain chemicals that can be harmful to dogs.

- Get your dog used to having his teeth handled by gently placing your finger in his mouth against his teeth. Carefully manipulate his lips so he gets used to the feeling.

- If you find he doesn't particularly like this, try dipping your finger in chicken broth or peanut butter so your dog learns to like the treatment.

- When you are ready to brush, place one hand over your dog's mouth and gently pull back his lips.

- Apply a small amount of toothpaste to the brush and rub it gently over a few of his teeth.

- After a few seconds, stop brushing and give your Bichon Frise a treat for good behavior.

- Slowly increase the length of your brushing sessions over a few days until your dog lets you brush all of his teeth in one session.

- In addition to brushing your Bichon Frise's teeth at home you should also make sure he gets a dental check-up from the vet every 6 months.

Chapter Seven: Vet Care Your Bichon Frise

Generally, this is a healthy dog. Just like other breeds, they are prone to certain health issues. If you are buying a puppy, make sure you buy from breeders with necessary health clearances. The health clearance is an indication that the dog has been tested and is cleared of certain deadly health conditions. They should get health clearances from recognized health institutions for elbow dysplasia, hip dysplasia, von Williebrand's disease, and hypothyroidism.

Common Health Issues

Bladder Infections

This can cause bladder stones including phosphorus, magnesium, and excessive protein in the diet. Take your Bichon to a veterinary doctor if he has difficulty urinating, bloody urine, loss of appetite or hugely affected by any of the viral or bacterial infection.

Allergies

Bichon can be afflicted with food allergies and contact allergies. They are very sensitive to fleabites. Take him to a veterinary doctor if you suspect that your Bichon is licking at his paws, scratching or rubbing his face consistently.

Patellar Luxation

This is a common health condition in small dogs- it means dislocation of a bone at a joint and/ or knee joint. This can lead to crippling. Experience has shown that most dogs lead relatively normal lives with this health condition.

Vaccination Sensitivity

Most Bichons are hugely affected by routine vaccinations and / or affected by this sensitivity. Symptoms includes, but not limited to soreness, facial swelling, lethargy and hives. Sometimes, a vaccine-sensitive dog can develop complications or even die. After your dog is being vaccinated, ensure you watch his behavior carefully afterwards and call the attention of your veterinary doctor if you spot anything unusual.

Hip Dysplasia

This is a very serious health issue. Some Bichons show signs of lameness and pain in one or both rear legs. While some dogs may not display any sign of discomfort. The most effective way of handling this issue is by undergoing an x-ray screening from a reputable veterinary hospital. Arthritis can develop as the dog keeps advancing in age.

Juvenile Cataracts

This health condition develops in relatively young Bichons, mostly those within the age bracket of 6 to 10 years. It is said to be hereditary.

First Aid

As the owner of a Bichon Frise dog it is a good idea to have at least a basic idea of canine first aid.

General first aid and its universal lesson is currently using the Acronym Dr's ABC. By memorizing this you have at least a basic idea of what to do if you ever find yourself in a first aid situation.

Danger

Remove the animal from any further danger, and be aware of danger to yourself in the situation.

Response

Check the response of the dog, is he conscious?

Summon help

Shout for help, ask someone to call the vet if possible.

Airway

Check the dog's airway, can he breathe Is there an obstruction

Breathing

At this point there may be a need to re-trigger breathing for the animal. Holding the mouth closed you can gently breath air into your dog's nostrils. Try to visualize the size of his lungs and not over inflate them, try to mimic how your dog would pant.

Cardiac compressions may be necessary at this point. The dog should be laid on his right side and the heart massaged in a similar way to CPR compressions for a human but carefully at a ratio of one breath to every two to five compressions depending on the size of the dog. The average Bichon Frise would be around three compressions per breath. The heart is approximately located in the chest area above his front left leg. They usually have a stronger beat on the left but can be felt on both sides.

The basic sequence for CPR is as follows:

1. Check for signs of breathing which should be noticeable around the chest or by placing your cheek to your dog's mouth.
2. Check for a pulse which if this is not noticeable around the heart area, can be felt via the femoral artery. This is located on either of the back legs, on the inside of the leg, near to the top of the leg. By feeling inside that area, if there was a pulse you would feel it quite strongly there. It will be worth you detecting that now, so that you know where to look and how it should feel.
3. If neither breathing nor pulse are detected, start chest compressions. With the heel of your hand, press reasonably firmly, but in the case of the Bichon Frise, not too firmly that you risk cracking a rib. Count about three compressions
4. Now move over to your dog's mouth/nose and steadily blow into both and you should see the chest expand.
5. Again, move over to the chest and compress three times again.
6. Keep repeating the sequence until he starts to breath.

Circulation

In an emergency, the dog's pulse and circulation will need to be checked. If bleeding is apparent then the wound will need to be put under pressure and elevated, if possible, in order to contain the bleeding.

After first aid has been carried out, the Bichon Frise should always be taken to see the vet as a matter of urgency.

There are some particular conditions that can develop very quickly can cause rapid health deterioration; which as a Bichon Frise owner it is important to be aware of. One of these is heat stroke or heat exhaustion.

Heat Exhaustion

Dogs can only pant to cool themselves as they don't sweat like people do; except to a certain extent from their paw pads.

In the warm summer months, it is vital to keep your dog away from hot sun. Because he only cools his body on the inside by taking air from his surroundings, the dog in excessive heat, loses the power to cool himself at all. This will quickly lead to heat exhaustion which can be a fatal condition.

Dogs should never be left in hot cars, full sun or hot areas from which they cannot escape.

The symptoms of heat exhaustion are as follows;

- Panting (however, dogs do this naturally anyway and in most cases is not indicative of a problem)
- Restlessness
- Loss of focus in the eyes
- Deterioration of consciousness

- Staggering
- Collapse

If you suspect that your Bichon Frise dog is overheating it is vital never to take the panicked action of immersing him in cold water, as this can cause shock or even heart failure. Remove the dog from full sun and either drape damp towels over his body or dribble water over him to cool his overheated body gently. When the body has overheated, then it is vital to get your dog checked by the vet for symptoms of long-term damage.

A relatively new invention in the dog equipment world is the cooling vest. It can be placed in water then put onto the dog in hot weather. The water wicks the heat away from the dog's body as a process of evaporation. If you believe that your dog is particularly susceptible to hot weather, then a cooling vest is a really good investment.

Another good idea for the warmer months is to provide your dog with a stock pot iced pop. Simply pour stock into a big bowl, add some treats of varying types and freeze the entire thing. Then on a hot day turn the ice pop out into the garden and allow your dog to lick away happily. You may want to place this on some sort of a tray in case the whole thing melts before he has chance to consume it.

Essential Exercise

Every Bichon Frise dog needs daily walks, and will certainly not be happy at home all day. The adult Bichon Frise ideally needs a good walk every single day or he may develop problem behaviors. These gentle, sweet natured dogs are generally well behaved. However, excess energy build-up can easily cause destructive or even aggressive behavior, to a certain extent.

Many dog behavior problems are sorted out very quickly when the dog's food is changed (food causing allergies or just poor food quality lacking necessary nutrients) and when the daily walks are increased in time and intensity. But many of the most problematic behaviors stem from a lack of suitable exercise.

If you are out at work for a full day then why not consider a doggy day care or professional dog walker for your Bichon Frise dog. A good professional canine caretaker will wear your dog out and meet his social needs all at once.

Please be aware that Bichon Frise puppies along with other puppy breeds, need to be broken in gently to exercise, as their bones are soft whilst they are still growing. Your regular, long walks will begin when your puppy is a few months old.

Visits to the Vet

It is important to take your Bichon Frise to the vet on a regular basis. Regular visits to the vet can allow you to treat any issues your Bichon Frise has in the early stages to avoid them having a negative impact on your Bichon Frise's health. I recommend scheduling to see your vet at least twice a year – however more frequent visits are advantageous in identifying health problems! It is more important to prevent the onset of disease rather than treat them once they occur. With each visit to the vet you should make sure that you get your dog weighed. By getting your dog weighed on a regular basis you will know if you are feeding it the correct sized portions.

Vaccinations

Though you may not be able to prevent your Cavachon from developing certain inherited conditions if he already has a genetic predisposition, there are certain diseases you can prevent with vaccinations. During the first few weeks of life, your Cavachon puppy relies on the antibodies he receives from his mother's milk to fend off infection and illness. Once his own immune system develops, however, you will be able to administer vaccines to prevent certain diseases like canine distemper, parvovirus, and rabies.

Vaccinations for dogs can be divided into two categories: core vaccines, and non-core vaccines. Core vaccines are those that every dog should receive while noncore vaccines are administered based on your dog's level of risk. Depending on where you live and how often your Cavachon comes into contact with other dogs, you may not need to administer any non-core vaccines. According to the AVMA, recommended core vaccines for dogs include: distemper, canine adenovirus, canine parvovirus, and rabies. Non-core vaccines include: coronavirus, leptospirosis, Bordetella bronchiseptica, canine parainfluenza, and Borrelia burgdorferi. You will need to speak to your veterinarian about non-core vaccines to determine which ones your Cavachon does and doesn't need. The rabies vaccine can be very stressful for dogs but, unfortunately, it is necessary in the United States due to the prevalence of rabies in wild animals. Rabies has been eradicated in the U.K. so dogs living in this area will not need rabies vaccines. Some veterinarians recommend that you only administer the rabies vaccine every three years. However, some states require an annual rabies vaccine, so be sure to check with your local council.

It is important to note however that a rabies vaccine should not be administered less than one month before or after a combination vaccine. The Cavachon that will be going into kennels may need to be immunized against canine kennel cough too. Most boarding establishments insist on it. Kennel cough immunization is via drops squirted up the dog's nose. It can be quite a stressful experience for dog and owner.

After the initial vaccination has been given, this is where the need for boosters becomes hazy. Some veterinarians state that a dog must get a booster every year whilst others think that it is a needless assault on the dog's immune system leaving the animal susceptible to illness. Although the yearly booster and associated parasite prevention chemicals are standard procedure, at present more veterinarians are questioning the need for it. This is because each of the treatments has an effect on the dog's immune system and may leave the dog susceptible to passing viruses, illnesses which grow within the body, or bacteria in the environment.

Please note: *Titre testing* is commonly practiced to establish whether a dog that has been immunized, is in need of a booster for a specific vaccine. This is carried out by a simple laboratory blood test. If sufficient antibodies are present, then there is no need to vaccinate with that specific vaccine. Once again, please note that regular, unnecessary vaccinating, can have an adverse effect on your dog's health. It would also constitute a waste of money.

Your veterinarian will be able to provide you with specific vaccination recommendations for your Cavachon but, for reference, you will find a "general" vaccination schedule for dogs below:

Recommended Vaccination Schedule			
Vaccine	Doses	Age	Booster
Rabies	1	12 weeks	Annually
Distemper	3	6 to 16 weeks	3 Years
Parvovirus	3	6 to 16 weeks	3 Years
Adenovirus	3	6 to 16 weeks	3 Years

Parainfluenza	3	6 weeks, 12 to 14 weeks	3 Years
Bordatella	1	6 weeks	Annually
Lyme Disease	2	9, 13 to 14 weeks	Annually
Leptospirosis	2	12 and 16 weeks	Annually
Canine Influenza	2	6 to 8; 8 to 12 weeks	Annually

Chapter Eight: Showing Your Bichon Frise Dog

Showing your Bichon Frise can be a wonderful experience for both you and your pet. In training your dog, you will develop a closer relationship with him, and your dog may enjoy the experience as well.

For purebreds like the Bichon Frise, there are many opportunities for show. One of the most prestigious dog shows in the United States is the Westminster Kennel Club Dog Show which is held in Madison Square Garden in New York City each year. This two-day show is an all-breed benched competition for conformation. In the U.K., one of the top dog shows for purebreds is Crufts. This show is open to all kinds of dogs including.

Showing Bichon Frise Dogs

As long as your Bichon Frise is at least six months old, and AKC or UK KC registered, has no disqualifying faults, it can be shown. Spaying is a grey area, as it has generally been considered that neutered dogs cannot be shown. This is not entirely true as the KC for example, has allowed such cases. You should check this with your local Kennel Club. Winning at your fist show is very difficult. There is much to learn about the show world, and you'll need to be very prepared before you start showing your Bichon Frise.

Bichon Frises are one of the easiest breeds to show. You will need to attend many dog shows before both you and your Bichon Frise give a polished performance. There are also professional dog handlers that could show your Bichon Frise for you.

To get more information on showing, you'll need to contact your local kennel club and see if they have any handling classes or when the next show is. These are informal and casual events where all dog owners learn. These include puppies, handlers, and even judges. Losses and wins at these matches should be taken lightly. Even at a serious show, dog handlers and owners should try not to get too serious. The results are the judge's decision.

When competing at a real AKC show, every time the judge chooses your Bichon Frise as the best male or female Bichon Frise, it does not mean he or she is a Champion. Your dog wins up to 5 points. This depends on how many other dogs it defeats.

How To Become an AKC Champion

Your Bichon Frise must win 15 points including 2 majors. This means defeating enough dogs to win 3 to 5 points at a time. As a competitor, you're allowed to enter any class that your Bichon Frise is eligible for: Puppy, Novice. American Bred, Bred by Exhibitor, or Open. The Best of Breed class is for dogs that are already Champions.

This is a brief example and rules can change from time to time. Please check your countries Kennel Club for the latest rule changes and updates.

What to Know Before You Show

If you plan to show your Bichon Frise dog, there are a few things you need to know before you register. The exact rules and requirements will vary from one show to another, so pay attention to specific requirements. Before you attempt to show your Bichon Frise, make sure your dog meets the following requirements:

- Your dog needs to be fully house-trained, and able to hold his bladder for several hours.

- Your Bichon Frise needs to be properly socialized, and able to get along well with both humans and other dogs.

- Your dog should have basic obedience training, and he should respond consistently to your commands and look to you for leadership.

- Your Bichon Frise should be even-tempered, not aggressive or hyperactive in public settings.

- Your dog needs to meet the specific eligibility requirements of whatever show you are participating in. There may be certain requirements for age, for example.

- Your Bichon Frise needs to be completely up to date on his vaccinations so there is no risk of him contracting or spreading disease among other dogs at the show.

In addition to considering these requirements, you also need to make sure that you yourself are prepared for the show.

The list below will help you to know what to bring with you on the day of the show:

- Your dog's registration information
- A dog crate and exercise pen

- Food and water bowls for your dog
- Your dog's food and treats
- Grooming supplies and grooming table
- Trash bags for cleanup
- Any medications your dog needs
- A change of clothes for yourself
- Food and water for yourself
- Paper towels or rags for cleanup
- Toys to keep your dog occupied

Preparing Your Dog for Show

Your preparations for the dog show will vary according to the type of show in which you have entered. If you enter an obedience show for example, perfecting your dog's appearance may be less important than it would for a conformation show. Before you even enter your dog into a show you should consider attending a few dog shows yourself to get a feel for it. Walk around the tent where the dogs are being prepared for show and pay close attention during the judging to learn what the judges are looking for in any given show. The more you learn before you show your own dog, the better off you will be. One of the most important things you need to do in preparation for a conformation show is to have your Bichon Frise properly groomed so that his coat is in good condition.

Follow the steps below to groom your Bichon Frise in preparation for show:

- The night before the show, give your Bichon Frise a thorough brushing then trim his nails and clean his ears as well.
- Give your dog a bath and dry his coat thoroughly before brushing him again.
- Once your dog is clean, you need to keep him that way. Have him sleep in a crate that night and keep him on the leash during his morning walk.
- The day of the show, brush your Bichon Frise's coat again.
- When you arrive at the show, keep your dog in his crate or in a fenced exercise pen so he doesn't get dirty.

When it comes time for judging, just remember that the main reason you are doing this is to have fun with your dog. Do not get too upset if your Bichon Frise does not win. Just take notes of ways you can improve for the next show and enjoy the experience you and your dog had together that day.

Chapter Nine: Breeding Your Bichon Frise

Breeding Checklist

Before planning to breed your Bichon Frise, ask and answer the following questions:

- Are the female and male Bichon Frise registered?
- Are the female and male champions in the show ring, competitions, trials or events?
- Are the male and female considered "show quality", i f not champions?
- Are the parents of the male and female champions in t heir respective areas?

- Are the male and female free from any genetic conditi ons, such as hip dysplasia, eye conditions, nervous disorders, or deafness?
- Are you financially able to afford the cost of the breed ing and pregnancy if there are complications? Some stud fees can be $500.00 and up, and vet bills can be several thousand dollars if there are complications.
- Are the male and female at least two years of age and mature enough to breed?
- Do you have the physical space and actual time neces sary to care for the female Bichon during pregnancy, and for the pups after they are born and before they go off to their new homes?
- Do you have the pups pre-sold before they are born?

Responsible breeders will research and answer each of the above questions and complete all necessary health and genetic background checks. Bichons with any history of genetic conditions should not be bred, even if they do not exhibit the conditions themselves. All Bichons can be "carriers" of a specific genetic condition and can pass it on to their puppies, thereby seriously placing the puppies at risk for potentially debilitating and even deadly conditions.

Finding the Perfect Partner for Your Bichon Frise

Besides ensuring that the Bichon Frise you are breeding your female to is healthy and free from genetic conditions, you should also consider their overall appearance and temperament. Bichons that appear to be poorly kept, are not well groomed, or have fleas or skin rashes, usually are from homes or kennels that are not caring and responsible breeders. No matter what the Bichon's pedigree may be, these males generally are not good breeding material. It is also very important to interact with the male Bichon and get to know their temperament. Temperament, just like appearances, is often similar between parents and puppies. Picking a male and female Bichon of similar temperaments is important to have the best possible outcome for the temperament of the puppy. Of course, how the puppy is raised and treated by its owners also has a very big im- pact on their development, but it does all start with the behaviors of the adults. Most people want a Bichon Frise that is intelligent, loyal, friendly, and obedient, yet also able to provide some protection as a watchdog. Interacting with the male and female Bichon will allow you to understand if they are, by nature, friendly and obedience, aggressive, timid, or even non-responsive to people.

When talking with the owner of the male Bichon, be sure to ask if they have been used for breeding purposes before and if there were any complications or problems, either in the breeding or with the puppies. If possible, check with the owner of the female to verify the information. Once you have found the perfect partner, the next step is to introduce the Bichon. If at all possible, try familiarizing the two with each other prior to the female's estrus or heat cycle. Females will come into heat every six to nine months, depending on the breed. Often owners may be unaware the female is in heat, especially if she is outdoors most of the time.

Close examination will show a swelling of the external reproductive tract along with a discharge. For most females, this discharge will be red and bloody looking for the first 10 days of the cycle, and then it will become clear between days 10 to 15. The female will only breed during the most fertile time of her 21-day cycle, which is when the discharge is clear. After the 15th day the swelling and discharge will gradually subside until the next cycle. Females will tend to clean themselves more and may be more aggressive or protective during their cycle. They are also more likely to attempt to get out of the yard especially if there are other male dogs in the area. Male dogs will also be very attracted to your yard and may try almost anything to get in to breed your female. Care must be taken to keep the female very secured and protect during this time to prevent an unplanned pregnancy.

A good rule of breeding is to never leave a female in heat outside alone, even in a fenced yard. Always provide supervision or have the female in a secure kennel or run. It is always important to supervise the breeding. Females may be highly aggressive and may turn on males if they are not ready to breed when the male is present. Always monitor the pair when they are together and be able to quickly intervene if it appears that there are problems during the mating. Taking the time to find the right partner is critical to both the health of the mother and puppies, as well as the overall improvement of the breed. Irresponsible breeding leads to genetically inferior Bichon in the future, lack of conformity to breed standards, poor health, and even horribly debilitating genetic conditions which may cause the puppies incredible pain and suffering.

Reputable breeders work to improve the breed by only breeding the best possible adult Bichon to produce high quality puppies. Females should only be bred every other year, at the maximum. Most breeders only breed females every two or three years, to minimize the stress placed on the female and to give her a chance to fully recover, weight and energy wise, before being bred again.

Pregnancy and Beyond

Once the mating is complete, the next step is to guarantee that the female Bichon Frise is pregnant. Unfortunately, many females will show the same signs whether they are pregnant or are "false pregnant". Usually a veterinarian can complete an abdominal palpation at about the 20 to 30-day mark after the breeding and actually feel the puppies. Fetal heartbeats can often be determined by ultra sound between the 20 and 25th day. Females will become heavier and lazier, may stop eating and go through periods of vomiting, or may have slight changes in behaviors and personalities between the fifth to eighth weeks. The average pregnancy time for most breeds is 62 days with puppies being born sometime between the 54-72nd day after the breeding.

Pregnant female Bichon Frises should be fed high quality dry kibble and should be closely monitored for any rapid increases or decreases in weight. They should be given a moderate amount of exercise, but should not be exercised strenuously or during hot periods in the day. Pregnant Bichon females should not jump or be encouraged to leap on or off of furniture, even if they used to do so. A set of doggy steps is a great way to help your dog get on and off the couch, without risking a jump and a fall. Do not supplement a pregnant Bichon's diet with supplements or vitamins, as this can cause abnormal growth in the puppies or even problems with calcium absorption and bone growth once they are born.

Before adding anything to the female's diet, speak with your vet. At about the middle of the second month (around day 45), the female should be switched to a high-quality puppy food that will provide all the extra nutrients that both the mother and puppies will need. Continue feeding the high-quality dry puppy food until instructed to discontinue by the vet. Many vets recommend feeding puppy food until after the puppies are weaned. The vet should see the female Bichon Frise at about the 20-30-day mark to confirm the pregnancy. He or she may then request that the female be brought back again at specific times or just if there are problems or concerns. Most females having their first litter or if there have been problems previously with a pregnancy, will re- quire constant monitoring by the vet. Females that have had a previous litter with no problems may not need as many regular check-ups, but should still be brought to the vet if anything appears abnormal.

One of the biggest problems to watch for is an infection of the uterus called pyometra that can occur in both pregnant and false pregnant females. A thick, smelly discharge from the vulva is usually the most obvious sign. This condition usually occurs four to eight weeks from the estrus cycle, and can usually be treated with antibiotics, if discovered early in the infection. If untreated, it is potentially life threatening to both the puppies and the female and immediate treatment is re- quired. Some females may not show any discharge but will stop eating, become listless and disinterested. Some females may require surgical removal of the reproductive tract if the condition is not treated.

Whelping

If this is your Bichon Frise's first pregnancy, consider talking to your vet in advance to find out how to contact him or her if there is an emergency. Be sure to ask if the vet will come to your home or if you have to bring your Bichon to the clinic if there is a problem. Most vets will come to your home, but it is always best to ask and find out for sure.

Generally, puppies will be born without assistance. However, some breeds are prone to whelping problems. Many of the miniature breeds and some of the small breeds will require assistance or even surgical removal of the puppies, called cesarean section. The vet should be prepared to provide these services. Calling when you know your Bichon is going into labor is the most important part of helping the vet to be ready.

The easiest way to tell if your Bichon Frise is going into labor is to start recording her temperature during the pregnancy. Take the temperature rectally, starting at about day 50. Keep a record of the reading, which is normally between 100 and 102.5 degrees F. Just before your Bichon is going into labor the temperature will drop down below 100 degrees. As soon as this drop occurs notify your vet and move her to the whelping area. Some females will also start to "nest" or build their own whelping den. Watch for the female digging, arranging bedding or blankets, or trying to get into closets or other confined spaces. The teats or nipples will also start to drip a milky substance in most females, especially if they have had a litter before.

Have a whelping box prepared that is large enough for the mother to be able to stretch out in. Remember this is where the puppies will be for the first three or four weeks so bigger is definitely better. Whelping boxes that are too small may squeeze the mother and puppies too tightly together leading to the potential of the mother smothering a puppy. Whelping boxes need to have sides that are low enough to let the mother step out of but high enough to keep the puppies in. Line the whelping box with towels or soft cotton sheets, something that is disposable, as it will become very soiled during the birth.

A discharge will appear from the female Bichon's swollen vulva. Usually shortly after this a puppy will appear, head first. Some puppies may be born hind end first, known as breach. This is not serious, unless the puppy becomes lodged or the female is straining excessively. Never grab the feet and pull on the puppy. Call the vet unless you are experienced with assisting in birthing puppies. Each puppy will be in his or her own placenta, or it will be expelled shortly after the puppy. The mother should immediate lick this off the puppy. She will also nip at the umbilical cord, but new mothers may not know to either clear the amniotic sac or nip the cord. Some towels, a pair of sharp scissors, and a child's nasal aspirator can be used to clip the cord, clear the fluids and rub the puppy dry. Always have a whelping box prepared that is large enough for the mother to be able to stretch out in. Remember this is where the puppies will be for the first three or four weeks so bigger is definitely better. Whelping boxes that are too small may squeeze the mother and puppies too tightly together leading to the potential of the mother smothering a puppy.

Whelping boxes need to have sides that are low enough to let the mother step out of but high enough to keep the puppies in. Line the whelping box with towels or soft cotton sheets, something that is disposable, as it will become very soiled during the birth. A discharge will appear from the female Bichon's swollen vulva. Usually shortly after this a puppy will appear, head first. Some puppies may be born hind end first, known as breach. This is not serious, unless the puppy becomes lodged or the female is straining excessively. Never grab the feet and pull on the puppy.

Call the vet unless you are experienced with assisting in birthing puppies. Each puppy will be in his or her own placenta, or it will be expelled shortly after the puppy. The mother should immediate lick this off the puppy. She will also nip at the umbilical cord, but new mothers may not know to either clear the amniotic sac or nip the cord. Some towels, a pair of sharp scissors, and a child's nasal aspirator can be used to clip the cord, clear the fluids and rub the puppy dry.

Always massage gently near the umbilical cord to stimulate breathing.

Generally, the first puppy will be born about 20 minutes or sooner after the mother begins to strain and push. If the first puppy is not born with 40 minutes call the vet for assistance. Females with more than one puppy may take several minutes to up to an hour or more between puppies. If the female is not straining but is resting, this is perfectly normal. If she is straining for more than 20 minutes after the first puppy call the vet immediately. Some female Bichons will make a lot of noise and howl and yelp whereas others may be relatively quiet. Check with your vet if you have any concerns about the female or her behavior. Once all the puppies are born the afterbirth will be expelled. If it does not clear from the female the vet should be called as this can lead to infections and other complications in the future. The female will continue to have a dark or colored discharge for several weeks after the delivery and that is normal. If the discharge appears the color of fresh blood immediately contact your vet.

As soon as the puppies are born, increase the female Bichon Frise's food intake as she will need extra nutrition for lactation. Some vets may recommend a calcium supplement at this time, whereas others may not. As before the birth, check with the vet regarding any supplements or products you are using on the female. Avoid any topical lotions, flea treatments or chemicals either in the female Bichon's diet or on her skin, as the chemicals will be passed to the puppies through the milk.

Special Notes on Breeding A Bichon Frise

At one time, the Bichon Frise had such stellar popularity that many turned to unethical breeding practices to keep up with the demand. This led to a dog that was not only physically inferior but worlds apart from its normally happy temperament. Nowadays, true Bichon Frise enthusiasts and those who professionally breed them are quite picky about who breeds what dogs, and where. Once defects of both a physical and temperamental nature are bred into a dog's line, it can take years to breed them back out. Those who breed champion Bichon Frises for show or for companionship keep very detailed records and pay very close attention to bloodlines.

Those who breed Bichon Frises as pets with no consideration to bloodlines and defects are not likely to be able to guarantee the quality of their pups. To guarantee the quality not only of the litter but the bloodline, a great majority of professional breeders screen their pups for such things as eye, hip and ear problems before allowing them to be adopted out. This means that a Bichon Frise adopted from a legitimate breeder will come with a genuine health certificate.

A good indicator of a less than scrupulous breeder is one that claims to breed and sell Teacup Bichon Frises. In all reality, there is no such thing. The average Bichon will weigh in at approximately seven pounds at its smallest. More often than not, a breeder in this type of situation is simply trying to pass off a Bichon with a defect in size. It is mostly likely a runt or is lacking in growth hormone production, a sign of more serious problems. An undersized dog presents a range of troubles with its internal organs and can end up costing an owner thousands of dollars in vet bills. Those breeders advertising Teacup Bichons should be avoided at all cost as they are passing on the chance for devastating defects; something the reputable breeder faithfully works against. A new issue in breeding to think about is shipping live animals versus onsite visits. Many breeders have begun using the internet to advertise their pups and then ship- ping them to buyers in distant locations. While it is convenient, it does not give a breeder a chance to see just who is adopting their Bichon Frise puppies. For those who are very attached to their work, this is simply not an option. An individual may present well with an application or over the phone, but there is no way to know for sure if that representation is truly accurate. Many breeders still require onsite visits to their kennels to evaluate potential buyers; or they may even require in home visits to ensure their pups are going to the right environment.

Registering the Puppies

Purebred Bichon Frise puppies should be litter registered as soon as they are born. This allows the organization, American Kennel Club, Canadian Kennel Club, Kennel Club (UK), or the Kennel Club in your country, to be able to recognize the registration that will come in from the owner at a later date. Be sure to register with the correct organization, as there are many registries that will be happy to register the litter but really mean nothing with regards to registering the Bichons as individuals later. To litter register the puppies, the breeder will require the information about the sire (father) and the dam (mother), and all other information regarding the place and date of birth. The AKC or kennel club will then send enough paperwork for each Bi- chon puppy to be sold with a litter registration certificate and the paperwork re- quired for the final registration. Breeders will include this with the sale of the puppy. Since most puppies are sold in advance, the breeder can fill in much of the information and provide assistance to the new owners on how to complete the process.

Chapter Ten: Other Care Needs

Bichon Frise Safety in Cars

Bichon Frises, like people, need to be secured when traveling in vehicles. Just like a person, a Bichon's weight can be enough to sustain injury in the event of an accident or a sudden stop. There are two main devices that can be used to restrain your Bichon Frise while in a vehicle. One of these devices is a crate or plastic kennel that can be fastened to the car seat using the car safety belt.

For Bichon Frises, a kennel is the most practical choice in a vehicle. A seatbelt style harness device can also be used to keep your Bichon Frise secure as it sits on the seat. These harness type devices are very comfortable and have padded straps to prevent any wear or rubbing. In addition, since they support the whole chest area of the Bichon Frise, in the event of a sudden stop or accident, their weight is not stopped by the neck, rather by the whole front section of the Bichon Frise.

Occasionally, a Bichon Frise will be in a car that is in an accident. If the dog is injured in a car, use the same basic first aid principles as you would for a person. Remove them from the vehicle and place them in a safe, dry area. Cover the Bichon with a blanket and try to keep them calm and relaxed. Apply a towel or bandage to any open cuts or bleeding areas. If you are unfamiliar with the Bichon a makeshift muzzle out a sock or piece of soft cotton material is a good safety device to pre- vent the frightened dog from biting you while you try to care for the injuries. Im- mediately seek a veterinarian's assistance.

Ventilation and Overheating

Sometimes, Bichon Frises are left unattended in cars in the heat of the day. Often, well-meaning pet owners park in the shade and even leave the windows rolled down a bit. People simply don't realize that the inside of a car can heat up incredibly quickly, even when parked out of the direct sun.

A Bichon's normal body temperature is between 101 and 102 degrees F. At between 105 and 108 degrees F, a Bichon's body will begin to shut down and death will occur almost immediately, as the body can no longer cool the internal organs and the brain. The temperature within a parked car can increase over 34 degrees per minute at an outside temperature of 95 degrees F, which provides little opportunity for a Bichon to be rescued.

Bichon Frises require constant ventilation and air circulation to be able to maintain their body temperature. You should plan to leave your Bichon at home or only run errands in the coolest times of the day, if you absolutely have to take your dog with you. If at all possible, consider taking your Bichon with you when you leave the car, or have a friend or family member come with you and leave the car running and the air conditioning on. Never leave a Bichon unattended in a running vehicle as they could accidentally put the car into gear.

Cold

Bichon Frises are small dogs that are not as capable of withstanding cold temperatures as other breeds. In fact, a small sweater when going out is a good idea for those dogs living in colder than average climates. The Bichon Frise will always need a warm dry place to stay free from wind, water or extreme temperatures. As they are a dog that spends much of their time inside, they will have far less tolerance for cold weather. Always use caution when exercising Bichons in extremely cold weather as this can damage their respiratory systems.

Conclusion

In essence, Bichon Frise is a cheerful and sociable breed that truly gives you joy while training them. This type of dog is good to have as a member of the household and they are considered pretty little pooches.

With the Bichon Frise's happy-go-lucky personality, the bouncy, playful and active pooch certainly delights everyone. This breed relates well with children and is friendly with other pets and strangers. They are the type of dog that is described as very responsive, sensitive and very affectionate. They love to be cuddled' however, they have the tendency to bark excessively and develop some behavior problems when left alone most of the time.

Bichons are certified very cheerful, an outstanding house dog and easy to live with. They love to snuggle into pillows and laps, loves to play games and sit atop of the couch so it can peep out the window.

This breed is especially recommended to people with allergies because they are regarded as hypoallergenic.

There are times when Bichons may be barky and reserved especially to strangers.

Bichons are likely to express their unhappiness by means of barking and destructive chewing.

Bichons are good pet for people with kids or those who reside in apartments as long as it is provided with sufficient exercise. They can live indoors and still stay active and they are all right without a huge yard to play on.

Several Bichons live long; however, unluckily they are susceptible to chewing and scratching themselves into terrible skin conditions. They are typically allergic to chemicals, pollen, fleas, grass and the like.

What makes Bichons a good pet is their strong desire to make humans especially their owners delighted.

The Bichon Frise does not have any trouble bonding with their new owner.

The Bichon Frise is known as one of the highest maintenance dogs across the world.

Hopefully you have have found the contents useful, informative and inspiring. There is a lot to consider when buying any dog, and consequently to appreciate their needs. Hopefully this book reflects that. For the most part, dogs that are properly looked after with love, care and respect, will repay you with unconditional love and devotion, many times over.

Thank you for reading!

Glossary of Dog Terms

Adoption – A process in which a rescued pet is placed into a permanent home.

Acute Disease – refers to a disease or illness that manifests quickly

Agility – This is a sport in which the dog handler guides and instructs the dog through a course of obstacles while being timed. Accuracy through this obstacle course is paramount. The dogs must complete the obstacle course without a leash or toys (or food) as incentives. The handler can only use voice, movement and various body signals in order to direct the dog.

AKC – American Kennel Club, the largest purebred dog registry in the United States

Almond Eye – Referring to an elongated eye shape rather than a rounded shape

Apple Head – A round-shaped skull

Balance – A show term referring to all of the parts of the dog, both moving and standing, which produce a harmonious image

Beard – Long, thick hair on the dog's underjaw

Best in Show – An award given to the only undefeated dog left standing at the end of judging

Bitch – A female dog

Bite – The position of the upper and lower teeth when the dog's jaws are closed; positions include level, undershot, scissors, or overshot

Blaze – A white stripe running down the center of the face between the eyes

Board – To house, feed, and care for a dog for a fee

Breed – A domestic race of dogs having a common gene pool and characterized appearance/function

Breed Standard – A published document describing the look, movement, and behavior of the perfect specimen of a particular breed

Buff – An off-white to gold coloring

Canine- a term for dog.

Canine Teeth- also known as eye teeth, the largest teeth found in the dog's mouth. They are long, curved teeth on either side of the mouth, top and bottom.

Chronic Disease – refers to a disease that will last indefinitely.

Clip – A method of trimming the coat in some breeds

Coat – The hair covering of a dog; some breeds have two coats, and outer coat and undercoat; also known as a double coat. Examples of breeds with double coats include German Shepherd, Siberian Husky, Akita, etc.

Condition – The health of the dog as shown by its skin, coat, behavior, and general appearance

Crate – A container used to house and transport dogs; also called a cage or kennel

Crossbreed (Hybrid) – A dog having a sire and dam of two different breeds; cannot be registered with the AKC

Dam (bitch) – The female parent of a dog;

Dock – To shorten the tail of a dog by surgically removing the end part of the tail.

Double Coat – Having an outer weather-resistant coat and a soft, waterproof coat for warmth; see above.

Drop Ear – An ear in which the tip of the ear folds over and hangs down; not prick or erect

Entropion – A genetic disorder resulting in the upper or lower eyelid turning in

Fancier – A person who is especially interested in a particular breed or dog sport

Fawn – A red-yellow hue of brown

Feathering – A long fringe of hair on the ears, tail, legs, or body of a dog

Groom – To brush, trim, comb or otherwise make a dog's coat neat in appearance

Heel – To command a dog to stay close by its owner's side

Hip Dysplasia – A condition characterized by the abnormal formation of the hip joint

Inbreeding – The breeding of two closely related dogs of one breed

Kennel – A building or enclosure where dogs are kept

Litter – A group of puppies born at one time

Markings – A contrasting color or pattern on a dog's coat

Mask – Dark shading on the dog's foreface

Mate – To breed a dog and a bitch

Neuter – To castrate a male dog or spay a female dog

Pads – The tough, shock-absorbent skin on the bottom of a dog's foot

Parti-Color – A coloration of a dog's coat consisting of two or more definite, well-broken colors; one of the colors must be white

Pedigree – The written record of a dog's genealogy going back three generations or more

Pied – A coloration on a dog consisting of patches of white and another color

Prick Ear – Ear that is carried erect, usually pointed at the tip of the ear

Puppy – A dog under 12 months of age

Purebred – A dog whose sire and dam belong to the same breed and who are of unmixed descent

Saddle – Colored markings in the shape of a saddle over the back; colors may vary

Shedding – The natural process whereby old hair falls off the dog's body as it is replaced by new hair growth.

Sire – The male parent of a dog

Smooth Coat – Short hair that is close-lying

Spay – The surgery to remove a female dog's ovaries, rendering her incapable of breeding

Trim – To groom a dog's coat by plucking or clipping

Undercoat – The soft, short coat typically concealed by a longer outer coat

Vaccine – a shot that is given to a dog to help produce immunity to a specific disease.

Wean – The process through which puppies transition from subsisting on their mother's milk to eating solid food

Whelping – The act of birthing a litter of puppies

Index

S

T

U

V

W

Photo Credits

https://www.canva.com/photos/MADO0ftDIC0-bichon-frise-being-lovingly-groomed/

Page 98, tsik via Canva.com (Canva Pro License)

https://www.canva.com/photos/MADBUTPZm98-cute-pure-breed-bichon-frise-puppy/

Page 110, cynoclub via Canva.com (Canva Pro License)

https://www.canva.com/photos/MAD2guBw6QY-young-bichon-frise/

Page 116, Lisa_Nagorskaya via Canva.com (Canva Pro License)

https://www.canva.com/photos/MADB_f_Piq4-bichon-frise/

Page 129, kosziv via Canva.com (Canva Pro License)

https://www.canva.com/photos/MADCTxtBcXQ-bichon-frise-looking-out-of-car/

References

Bichon Frise- Dogtime.com

https://dogtime.com/dog-breeds/bichon-frise#/slide/1

Bichon Frise- Dogbreedinfo.com

https://www.dogbreedinfo.com/bichonfrise.htm

Bichon Frise Dog Breed Profile – Purina.com

https://www.purina.com/dogs/dog-breeds/bichon-frise

Bichon Frise- Dailypaws.com

https://www.dailypaws.com/dogs-puppies/dog-breeds/bichon-frise

Bichon Frise – Petcoach.co

https://www.petcoach.co/breed/bichon-frise

Bichon Frise Grooming– Espree.com

https://www.espree.com/BreedProfiler/bichon-frise-grooming-bathing-and-care

Grooming Your Bichon Frise – Pethelpful.com

https://pethelpful.com/dogs/DIY-Bichon-Frise-Grooming

Adopting a Bichon Frise – Animalplanet.com

http://www.animalplanet.com/pets/5-things-you-should-know-before-you-adopt-a-bichon-frise/

Bichon Frise – Vetstreet.com

http://www.vetstreet.com/dogs/bichon-frise

Bichon Frise – Petplan.co.uk

https://www.petplan.co.uk/pet-information/dog/breed/bichon-frise/

Bichon Frise Dog Breed Information and Personality Traits – Hillspet.com

https://www.hillspet.com.ph/dog-care/dog-breeds/bichon-frise

Crate Training – Bichon.org

https://bichon.org/crate-training-how-to-do-it-and-why-it-is-important/

Bichon Frise – All-about-bichon-frises.com

https://all-about-bichon-frises.com/how-to-train-a-puppy/basic-dog-obedience-training/

Bichon Frise Dog Training and Bichon Frise Breed Information – Dog-obedience-training-review.com

https://www.dog-obedience-training-review.com/bichon-frise-training.html

Bichon Frise – Akc.org

https://www.akc.org/dog-breeds/bichon-frise/

Bichon Frise Traning– Petcareeducation.com

https://petcareeducation.com/bichon-frise-training/

Bichon Frise Dog Training and Bichon Frise Breed Information – Dog-obedience-training-review.com

https://www.dog-obedience-training-review.com/bichon-frise-training.html

How to Breed Bichon Frise– Breedingbusiness.com

https://breedingbusiness.com/how-to-breed-bichon-frises/

Bichon Frise– Dogzone.com

https://www.dogzone.com/breeds/bichon-frise/

www.ingramcontent.com/pod-product-compliance
Lightning Source LLC
Chambersburg PA
CBHW060858280326
41934CB00007B/1104